The Art
Mental
Toughness

Build Grit, Destroy Negativity, and Develop the Resilience to Achieve Long Term Goals

By Hung Pham
http://www.missionandpossible.com

Your Free Gift

As a way of showing my gratitude, I'm offering a resource that's exclusive only to you.

>> CLICK HERE for Your FREE eBook on the 5 Key Strategies I Used to Turn My Life Around

It's tough not to feel lost in life. The secret is to find out what changes are needed and how to make those changes. In my free eBook, I'll show you how to:

- Remove self-limiting beliefs using this one simple trick
- Stop worrying about the future so that you can focus on the present
- Find the best advice on what to do in your current situation

- Stop living in the past and how to start moving forward
- Appreciate your life more by reframing your thinking
- And much more

>> CLICK HERE to download your FREE eBook now!

THE ART OF MENTAL TOUGHNESS: BUILD GRIT, DESTROY NEGATIVITY, AND DEVELOP THE RESILIENCE TO ACHIEVE LONG TERMS GOALS

Introduction

The word "potential" as defined by Merriam Webster's dictionary is

"Existing in possibility or capable of development into actuality."

Children who are well prepared at an early age have a higher potential for academic success. Athletes who spend more time training and taking care of their bodies have a higher potential for personal success when they compete.

I like to think of potential as the natural ability for growth, development, and future success. It's about:

"Being the best we can be."

If you read a lot of personal or self-development books, you'll hear the term potential thrown around a lot. It's almost to the point of sounding too cliché. But for me, finding your true potential is all about taking the action to be better every day.

But how many of us have discovered what our true potential is? How many of us are using it to become successful? I know I wasn't and it was due to one simple fact.

The self-limiting beliefs I created for myself were holding me back.

That's why I wrote this book, to destroy the self-limiting beliefs that keep each, and every one of us back from being our best selves. My goal is to help you build and achieve mental toughness.

For most of my 20's I struggled with finding my identity. I changed jobs every two or three years because that's what I was told to do to avoid being stagnant. I took jobs for more money and a better title because I thought that's how career advancement worked.

Then when I turned 30, I started to question what my purpose really was in life. I had a well-paying job, yet I couldn't help wondering why was I so miserable. I wanted to move forward, but for some reason, I felt trapped.

I started comparing myself to other people. If I couldn't keep up with my peers I would regularly beat myself up over, and over again. I started to question the decisions I made instead of trusting my gut. With every mistake came regret and doubt.

I couldn't help feeling that something was missing in my life, despite people telling me that I was doing well. I just knew that this wasn't the life I wanted for myself. I began to ask:

"Is this what success is?"

I would spend the next several years trying to answer that very question. Everything I did, every tough decision; every sacrifice I made was to help bring me one step closer to finding the true meaning of success.

The contents of this book have all come from my own personal experience. I've spent many hours documenting every step in the process so that I can share it with you. They are all tried and true.

"Break Through" focuses on breaking down the self-limiting beliefs that hold us back from success. It also focuses on discovering our passion and helps you to understand where you are today and where you want to be tomorrow.

It teaches you how to project all your ambitions and goals to your external world and bring it to life. It's about becoming a better person every day; better than the person you were yesterday.

For best results, read through this once from beginning to end. The chapters are written so that you begin with unlocking your true potential mentally and then taking action to create change in your physical world.

Here's to breaking the mental chains that hold you back and achieving your potential!

Step 1: Understand How Beliefs Works

It all starts with a thought; an electrical signal that travels from your brain throughout your body. It carries with it messages used to communicate to the receptors and cells of other limbs, organs, and body parts.

As you're reading this book now, millions of electrical signals are being sent to help you see, absorb, and formulate the words.

And all of this happens in a blink of an eye.

This is the power of the mind and what you choose to believe.

A belief is what we believe to be true. It is formed through a series of repeated thoughts. They are only true because we believe it to be true, not what others believe to be true.

When the great explorer Christopher Columbus lived, many people believed the world to be flat. They believed that once you go off a waterfall, you fall off the face of the Earth.

Columbus, on the other hand, believed the world to be round. He had to fight all the foolish beliefs that the world was flat in order to get men to sail around the world with him.

The world being round was his belief.

Imagine going out on a Friday night with your friends. You happen to see that cute girl from across the bar with her friends.

You want to talk to her but before you can muster up the courage, a range of thoughts pop into your head. You begin to think:

"Is she single?"

"Will she find me attractive?"

"How can I talk to her without coming off as desperate?"

"She probably has a boyfriend; she's too cute to be single."

"Maybe she doesn't, and I'm just overthinking it."

"I'll just wait here until she sees me."

"Forget it; she's out of my league. Why bother and get rejected?"

Before you know it, the bar is closing. As you scramble to look for her, she's nowhere to be found. You realize you might never see her again and let a perfectly good opportunity slip through your hands.

Why didn't you go up and talk to her the minute you saw her?

Why did you wait so long?

In that example, your beliefs were protecting your feelings. Instead of pushing yourself to talk to this girl, your beliefs talked you out of it. They were protecting you from feelings of fear, rejection, and disappointment.

Although you might have protected your ego from rejection, you didn't protect your heart from being disappointed.

Sometimes your beliefs give you a false understanding of what is actually true and sometimes they can cause harm.

Let's look at a real-life example.

If you've read my other books *"Restart Your Life"* or *"Finding Purpose"*, then you're probably familiar with my story. If not, let me give you a quick summary.

During my 20's I suffered from a serious gambling addiction that led to severe depression. Over the course of eight years, I estimate I lost over 250K dollars. At my lowest, I even thought about taking my own life.

That's how miserable I was.

Now it wasn't like I gambled the entire duration of those eight years. There were many times where I tried to quit but didn't have enough willpower. More importantly, my beliefs kept me oppressed.

I believed that I deserved everything that was happening to me. I was in debt for over 50K dollars, I had no money in my bank account, and cried because I didn't think I would ever find a solution.

I believed that I would end up alone because nobody would ever want to be with someone like me. Heck, I wouldn't even want to be with someone like me. Whenever I tried to quit gambling, I gave up as soon as it got hard. I kept thinking that my life would never to improve.

And that's when the suicidal thoughts crept in:

"You're a failure, a waste of a life."

"Nobody will ever want to be with you."

"Maybe you should just end it, so you don't have to keep disappointing others."

My beliefs were preventing me from moving forward. But the scariest part was that they allowed me to think about taking my own life. They were enabling me to do the unthinkable.

My beliefs existed because I gave them life. I believed them to be true and as a result, they oppressed me. My beliefs became self-limiting beliefs. They were the reason why I struggled for as long as I did.

It wasn't until I decided to challenge those self-limiting beliefs, did I finally make progress. That's when I saw the opportunity to realize my potential. That's when I began to break through.

What are some of your self-limiting beliefs? Have you tried challenging them before? If not, continue reading and I will show you how.

Step 2: Find Out Where Self-Limiting Beliefs Come From

We all have self-limiting beliefs; some of us more than others. I don't think anyone is immune to them. To destroy our self-limiting beliefs, it is important first to understand where they come from.

Take, for example, two children growing up together. One is a boy, the other a girl, and they are both the same age. At some point in their development, the boy begins to play with robots and LEGO while the girl is conditioned to play with dolls and stuffed animals.

The boy grows up and excels at STEM (science, technology, engineering, and math) subjects in school while the girl struggles in those same subjects. As a result, the boy graduates college with a computer science degree and earns a high paying job as an engineer.

The girl, believing she is not smart enough to develop her STEM skills, is pushed to explore non-technical professions that are significantly lower in salary and earning potential. She accepts that she is not smart enough to apply for technical occupations.

Is she correct to think this way or do her self-limiting beliefs oppress her?

According to NPR.org, during the rise of computers; the period between 1970 and 1980, the number of women studying computer science were growing faster than men.

However, in 1984, something changed. The number of women studying computer science started decreasing steadily. While there are no definitive answers, many believed this was caused by the introduction of the personal computer.

Do you remember Apple's iconic 1984 commercial? If not, take two minutes and search for it on YouTube. That was the commercial that would change the landscape of personal computing.

As more and more computers were introduced to households, you couldn't really do much outside of some word processing and play video games. The notion that computers were made for boys became the narrative; it became the belief.

And through that belief, we accepted that boys should be playing on computers and not girls. This wasn't something that was scientifically determined. It was a marketing narrative that was repeatedly beat into our minds.

And we accepted.

Girls have every right to play with robots and LEGO and excel at STEM subjects in school. Women have every right to study computer science and become engineers. The reason why more girls and women don't is because of the self-limiting beliefs that they have been subjected to.

Rarely do we create our own self-limiting beliefs. They are usually formed as a result of something happening to us or influencing how we think. To destroy our self-limiting beliefs, we must understand they come from external sources.

When you look at your own self-limiting beliefs, take a look deep down and find what the external source is. What event or action caused you to create the self-limiting belief?

It's time to challenge your self-limiting beliefs. Are you ready? If so, let's move on to the next chapter.

Step 3: Challenge Your Self-Limiting Beliefs

Just because you believe something about yourself doesn't necessarily make it true. Only when you repeatedly tell yourself that a belief is true, does it increasingly becoming a self-fulfilling prophecy. You subconsciously bring it to life.

If you believe you don't have what it takes to be an entrepreneur, you will make all types of excuses why you can't:

"It's not the right time."

"I'm too busy right now. Maybe when things die down."

"One day, I'm still working through a few potential ideas."

"I'm too old. I can't compete with those Stanford graduates."

In the previous chapter, we talked briefly about getting to the cause of your self-limiting beliefs. In this chapter, we're going to challenge them. The way to destroy your self-limiting beliefs is to question the validity.

It takes time to destroy these beliefs, and so the first thing that you have to do is challenge them, see if they really are true. There are a few ways to do so, but I'll cover my top three techniques.

Technique #1- Role Play

I'm not a fan of public speaking. There was an incident in junior high where I gave a report in front of class. I started to speak but about fifteen seconds in, I froze. Instead, I started laughing hysterically because I didn't know what else to do.

My teacher didn't think it was funny and scolded me in front of the class. Then she proceeded to give me an F on the report. Ever since then, I hated public speaking. As I got older and had to give more presentations, I never got used to it.

In 2015 I organized a conference on how to build better culture in the workplace. As much as I hate public speaking, being the founder, I needed to give the opening remark. I was terrified.

As I spent weeks practicing my ten-minute speech by myself, it wasn't enough to prepare me to speak in front of 200 people. I needed more. Unless I was speaking in front of hundreds of people, there wasn't a way to simulate the real thing.

Then on the day of the conference, about ten minutes before I was scheduled to speak, I closed my eyes and took a deep breath. I wasn't myself anymore. Instead, I was an actor playing a role. I played the role of an experienced speaker oozing with charisma and confidence.

I saw myself get on stage and lift the entire room up with my energy. I emulated every movement, hand gesture, and posture as if I was Tony Robbins. As I opened my eyes, I was no longer oppressed by my fear of public speaking. That's because I wasn't me anymore, I was playing another role.

As I got on stage for my opening remark, I rocked it.

The next time you're faced with a self-limiting belief, use it as an opportunity to see yourself in a role that would challenge that self-limiting belief. Envision it such that you embody everything about that newly created role.

Be in the moment and challenge your self-limiting belief.

Technique #2 – Write it Down

Whenever I get stuck and frustrated by a self-limiting belief, I take out a sheet of paper and write down reasons why my self-limiting belief is false. Sometimes you have to see it visually, and this is a great way to do so.

Let's say you're struggling to find the right partner to settle down with. In your mind, you tell yourself that you're not dating material. You believe that you have nothing to offer and therefore you don't deserve better.

Now write down on a sheet of paper all the qualities about yourself that you are proud of. Perhaps your list looks like this:

- I'm funny
- I'm loyal
- I'm affectionate
- I'm responsible
- I'm thoughtful
- I have a good head on my shoulders

When you're done, I want you to look at the list you just wrote and ask yourself the following:

"Would I want to settle down with someone who possesses these qualities?"

I'm sure you know the answer to this, but if this were me, yes those are all great qualities to have in a partner.

When in doubt, write it down.

Technique #3 – Reverse Your Thinking

So far, we've talked about how beliefs are formed and manifested in our lives. Continuing with the same approach, I want you to reverse your thinking on whatever your self-limiting belief is.

If you don't think you are fearless, I want you to start believing you are fearless.

If you don't have what it takes to be a leader, I want you to believe that you are already a leader.

If you are scared of taking risks in your career, I want you to adopt the mindset that you are meant for greatness.

Whatever your self-limiting belief is, flip it on its head and challenge it. A word of caution here. Just because you reversed your thinking once doesn't mean that the belief has changed.

Like any belief, it needs to be repeated so that you subconsciously bring it to life. It has to be engraved in your mind such that it becomes your truth. When it becomes your truth, it will influence your behaviors and actions in a positive manner.

Step 4: Find Your Voice in a Noisy Mind

How do you define a voice?

Is it the sound that comes out of our mouths when we speak? What about the sound in your head as you read this book? Is that my voice speaking to you or your voice repeating the words I've written?

Your voice is one of the most important forms of communication. I'm not referring to the sound you make when you speak. I'm talking about speaking, writing, composing music, making art, or some other form of self-expression.

Your voice is critical because it expresses who you are and what you believe.

Think of a time when you were a child playing with your favorite you at the time. My favorite toys growing up were Transformers. Close your eyes and picture it. Do you remember the feeling?

We find our voice at a very early age in the form of our imagination. Our imagination that brings inanimate objects, like toys, to life. As a child, I always used my imagination to create an entirely new world around me.

And because of my imagination, I was always entertained.

Now try to think of the last time you used your imagination as an adult?

Not so easy is it?

That's because as we get older, our mind receives interference from outside sources and distractions like opinions and expectations. We begin to either lose our voice or our voice becomes someone else's instead.

This is what I call noise.

Noise can appear in many forms. Some of the most familiar ones are:

- Living your life based solely on what your family, friends, and peers expect of you

- Living your life based on how society thinks you should live

- Making life decisions based on material factors instead of intrinsic ones

- Allowing self-doubt to prevent you from taking action when you need it most

- Trying to keep up with the "Joneses."

The more noise we encounter, the harder it is to find our voice. And without your voice, you lose touch of your purpose thus making it difficult to find your path.

How do you find your voice in such a noisy world?

Think back to any great action or adventure movie that you've ever seen. There's always a hero, a villain, and some epic quest that the hero embarks on to save the world; even if it means risking death.

One of my favorite movies of all time is The Matrix. Not only is the cinematography amazing but the storyline resonates with me.

There was a time in my life where I had a choice of either the red pill (harsh reality) or blue pill (blissful ignorance). I chose the red pill because I was determined to change reality no matter how bleak it seemed.

It was more important for me to change something real than to live in something fake.

The questions I asked myself were:

What is my epic quest?

What makes me angry?

How do I plan on saving the world?

I was tired of trying to live up to expectations that weren't mine. I was fed up with what other people expected of me. I knew what I wanted out of life, and I was ready to go after it.

To find my voice again, I needed to block out distractions. Anyone who had an unwarranted opinion on how I should live my life was ignored. I knew my life best, so why would I listen to someone who had no idea what I was going through?

I then searched for those who understood where I wanted to go; those who were already there and could offer me guidance. That's how I regained my voice, and my suggestion would be for you to do the same.

Step 5: Quiet Your Inner Critic

In 2012 I entered a startup workshop competition called Lean Startup Machine. The premise was that you and your team had 54 hours to come up with an idea, build a prototype, and find as many ways to validate it as you can.

Validation meant that it was an idea that solved a real problem, a real pain that people will pay for. For the workshop, validation can come in many forms such as cash, letters of intent, signed contracts, or tons of email signups for your product.

This was the first time I had done an event like this and was beyond terrified. The first 30 minutes of the competition was dinner and networking. I avoided trying to make small talk with anyone there.

Why? Because I didn't think I was good enough and I was scared. What did I know about startups when I had never started anything before? What value did I have to add to any conversation?

The competition started on a Friday night. Little did I know that by Sunday evening I was going to be crowned the winner of an idea that went on to raise 750K in funding.

However, none of this would've been possible if I hadn't quiet the inner critic inside of me.

Who exactly is this inner critic?

We all have an inner critic. In fact, we've had to listen to this inner critic at one point or another in our lives. The inner critic is harsh and likes to judge.

The inner critic often makes us have self-doubt, low self-esteem and is constantly undermining our self-confidence. The inner critic can permanently destroy us if we let it.

That is why it's important to quiet your inner critic.

When I avoided talking to people at the startup competition, it wasn't because I was inferior to them. It was because my inner critic was making me feel inferior. My inner critic was telling me I wasn't good enough; it didn't want me to succeed.

In fact, nobody's inner critic wants him or her to succeed.

But for me to make it through the weekend, I knew I had to quiet my inner critic. The first thing I did was to go to the bathroom and splash some cold water on my face.

Then I started coaching myself using the following steps below:

1. **State the obvious:** I knew I had no prior experience building a company or launching a product. But as I got to know more people during the weekend I found out neither did

anyone else. By stating the obvious, I was quick to get over my fear.

2. **Positive affirmations:** My inner critic was made up of all the negative self-limiting beliefs I had. Quieting my inner critic meant I had to replace those beliefs with positive affirmations. I had to believe that I belonged. Even if I wasn't as talented some of the people there, I still believed I could work just as hard or even harder than them.

3. **Quiet your inner critic with every win:** Throughout the weekend, the mentors would come by now and then to check on our progress. With every positive feedback, every win, I used it as an opportunity to quiet my inner critic. The more wins I got, the more confident I felt.

When I came to the event on Friday night, my inner critic was doing everything in his power to make me feel like I didn't belong. By Sunday evening, my inner critic was nowhere to be found.

That's because I finally silenced it by winning the competition. My team and the product we built over the weekend got so much validation the judges declared us the winners by a landslide over the next team.

It was such an amazing feeling. I remember thinking back to how nervous I was entering the competition and when it was over, I felt accomplished. I had proven to myself that I belonged. I wasn't sure if I would become a successful entrepreneur, but I gained the confidence to try.

None of this would've been possible if I didn't quiet my inner critic. Had I continued to listen to it, I would've never gotten out of that bathroom.

We all have inner critics; it's that little voice inside of our heads that likes to judge and create doubt whenever we are unsure of ourselves. But it's how we deal with our inner critic that determines whether we become successful or not.

The next time your inner critic tries to pass judgment on you, use the steps above to silence it.

Step 6: Plant the Seeds of Success

Think about what type of meaningful work you want to do in your life. Chances are, you haven't had much experience doing the type of work you want to do. It's not uncommon to feel this way.

Usually, when this happens, we have a habit of talking ourselves out of pursuing meaningful work. There's always some excuse like:

"Bad timing."

"Not ready."

"Too soon to tell."

I'm going to let you in on a little secret. There's never such thing as perfect timing. If there's something you want to do, you should start doing it. If you're not ready, at least begin putting in the work and preparation.

Before I decided to take the leap and become an entrepreneur, I spent years researching what successful people, in general, do.

I studied how they started their mornings and what their daily routines were. I paid attention to how they communicated and inspired others around them. I was determined to find out what made them successful.

This was my process for planting the seeds of success.

Successful people are successful for a reason. They think, walk, and talk differently than most people. What may seem like an obstacle to most of us, successful people see it as an opportunity.

But success is also subjective. What is considered success to one person might differ to another.

Just so we are clear, let me define what success means to me.

Success isn't about having a lot of money. Having lots of money can be a result of being successful, but it doesn't make a person successful; especially not the kind of success I'm passionate about.

To me, success is about creating positive change in the world. It's about having the freedom to pursue your dreams, create a long-lasting legacy, and add value to the lives of others. Success is about inspiring people to be better every single day.

That's how I define success. And yes, it's completely okay to be wealthy, as long as you focus on your key success goals.

This chapter is dedicated to all the things I've learned about being successful and planting the seeds of success.

Here are my top 10 tips to plant your seeds of success:

1. **Value your time:** Time is something we don't have an abundance of. It's also the one thing you can never get back. How you use your time today will determine how successful you are tomorrow.

2. **Be solution focused:** Successful people rarely complain. Rather than worrying about problems, they focus on finding solutions. Be a part of the solution, not the problem.

3. **Create a balanced life:** It can be easy to get lost in your work but don't neglect your physical, mental, and emotional health. Success is a marathon and having a balanced life enables you to be in it for the long run.

4. **Finish what you start:** It's always easy to start something new. You're excited and filled with adrenaline, but guess what's better than starting new projects? Finishing what you started.

5. **Take care of your body:** As you get older, your body needs more care and attention. Make sure you eat well, exercise, and get plenty of rest. Finding time to take care of your body isn't a sign of laziness; it's a sign of planning for the longevity.

6. **Set deadlines:** It can be tempting to say *"I'll get to it next week,"* or *"I'll do that someday,"* but if you really want to get things done, set deadlines for your tasks. Put a date and make it official.

7. **Learn to prioritize:** It can be tempting to have several projects going on at once; in fact, I held three jobs for a while. What helped me juggle everything is learning to prioritize. You need to prioritize the items that are going to be the most beneficial for you so you can focus most of your energy on one or two things.

8. **Understand the power of "no":** It's amazing how one word can improve

your life. Say no to people that are toxic, activities that add no value, and anything that takes away from your personal goals. Learn how to say no effectively.

9. **Enrich the lives of others:** Successful people know that they can't do it alone. Whether it's employees, peers, or friends and family, think about how you can enrich the lives of others. In return, they will enrich your life.

10. **ABC – Always Be Creating:** If you've ever watched the movie Glengarry Glen Ross, then you should know Alec Baldwin's famous line, *"A-always, B-be, C-closing."* Well, I'm here to tell you those ABC's are old school. The new ABC's of success is to Always Be Creating.

    Start a blog, write a book, create a YouTube video, or develop an iPhone application. Whatever it is, always push to create new opportunities for yourself.

Whether you work on all ten of these tips or just one at a time, commit to working on them until it becomes a part of your routine. Avoid the one and done syndrome. These aren't items to be checked off on a checklist.

The sooner you plant the seeds of success, the sooner you can reap the benefits.

Step 7: Build Your Personal Brand

When I was a child, I remembered pointing and screaming every time we drove by a McDonald's. As soon as I saw those large golden arches against a bright red background, something in my mind triggered feelings of happiness, excitement, and euphoria.

That's because I grew up eating happy meals. Both of my parents worked so eating fast food was a staple in our family. The food was good but what I loved most about the happy meal was the toy. Because of this, my mind associated the McDonald's logo with food and a toy every time I saw it.

Fast-forward 30 years later, and the same thing still happens whenever I drive my little nieces and nephews around. As soon as they catch the McDonald's logo outside the car window, they get excited.

That is the power of branding.

A brand is anything that invokes a feeling, a message, or a statement. A brand can be a design, a name, a symbol, or even a reputation. In the business world, a brand helps to create an identity that resonates with customers.

Think of some of the most famous brands in history. What comes to mind when I say, "Apple, Hostess, Nike, Southwest, or Starbucks?" All of these companies have created an iconic brand that we associate with a feeling, message, or statement.

When I think of Nike, I think of elite athletic performance.

When I think of Apple, I think of beautiful design and innovation.

But branding isn't exclusive to businesses only; people can have personal brands too. This is known as your reputation. What do people say when they are asked about you?

Are you dependable? Are you trustworthy? Do you have a reputation for being a good person?

Before the advancements in technology, our brand was built on how we interacted with others at a local level. Your reputation didn't expand beyond a circle of friends of friends.

However, in the digital age we live in, platforms such as Facebook, Twitter, Instagram, and LinkedIn have made it easier to build our personal brand on a larger scale.

Why is your personal brand important to your success?

For starters, your personal brand is not immune to your self-limiting beliefs. If you lack self-confidence, your personal brand will suffer and show it.

Building a recognizable personal brand can create many professional opportunities for you now and in the future. This can be dream job offers, new clients for your business, or recognition in your industry.

Your personal brand is the impression you want to leave in the minds of others. It is how you market yourself and your abilities. Your personal brand is a promise to your customers.

To start building your personal brand, I recommend the following steps:

1. **Conduct a personal landscape analysis:** To craft how you want your personal brand to be, it's important to know what your current brand is. You do this by conducting a personal landscape analysis.

    A personal landscape analysis gives you a sense of what others think or feel about you today. Start by asking your family, friends, and peers the following questions:

a. What do you do better than anyone else?

b. What do they see as your strengths?

c. What values do you believe in that others fail to exhibit?

d. What do they see as your weaknesses?

e. What are your negative habits (for example, do you have a short temper or are you poor at handling stress)?

f. Do you have personality traits that hold you back?

Ask them to be completely honest with you, so you can highlight the positives and work on the negatives.

2. **Create your personal brand vision:** To create your personal brand vision you'll have to start by answering the following four questions:

a. What is your life's mission? (What you see for yourself in the future)

b. What is your purpose? (What role you are going to play to bring your vision to life)
c. What are your values? (The principals that are important to you that you can never compromise)
d. What are your passions? (The things that get you out of bed every morning)

The purpose of these questions is to give you a framework with which to build your brand. Going forward your personal brand vision should drive what you do and the choices you make for yourself.

3. **Define your audience:** For your personal brand to be effective, you have to know exactly whom it is you want to target. Let's say you have a passion for social media and want to brand yourself as a social media expert.

Simply stating you are a social media expert isn't clear enough. Potential customers will have a hard time figuring out if you are right for them or not. You need to make the connection between who you are and what your target audience needs.

If you want to focus on independent businesses like restaurants or shop owners, a better way to reposition yourself is to say you are a social media expert that focuses on helping local small businesses build their presence on the Internet.

This way it's clearer who your target audience is and what they will gain by working with you. Rather than trying to serve everybody, you'll gain more success by focusing on a just a few target audiences.

4. **Create your digital footprint:** Once you've created your personal brand vision and identified who your target audience is, it's time to start putting yourself out there.

    I would highly recommend creating a professional website and/or blog for yourself. Platforms like Wordpress and Tumblr make it very simple to start blogging.

For a professional website, I highly recommend Strikingly. I use Strikingly myself and love it. It has a very simple, clean, sleek design and you don't need to be super technical to use it.

With so many social media tools out there, such as Facebook, Twitter, Linkedin, and Instagram how do you know which tool is right for building your personal brand?

The short answer is to try all of them.

Each tool has its own unique benefits and values. I won't go into all the details in this book, but my recommendation is to try all of them and see which one works best for you and your lifestyle.

Your goal for building your personal brand is to tell your story. Who you are, what you're about, and what people can expect from working with you.

It'll take some time in the beginning to get started, but once you get going, you'll understand the importance of branding and how it relates to your success.

Step 8: Nourish and Grow Your Professional Network

Upon graduating, every job I got was through hard work and sheer determination. My college didn't have a high-quality alumni network that I could tap into for job leads. I had to work for every opportunity that came my way.

However, even hard work and determination can only get you so far.

This is where having a powerful professional network at your disposal can take you to the next level. The great thing about having a powerful network is that anyone is capable of building one. You don't need to go to an Ivy League college, or even college for that matter, to build one.

To me, having a powerful network is one of the greatest career equalizers.

Do you remember the saying?

"It's not what you know; it's who you know."

While it may sound like someone complaining because his or her career isn't progressing, there is some truth to the saying.

Having a powerful network can be beneficial for the following reasons:

- **Career Opportunities** – the best jobs aren't the ones that are listed on job boards or company websites. They are usually the ones that come through a well-maintained network.

- **Guidance** – whether you're just entering the workforce or looking to change careers, having a strong network means that you'll have guidance throughout your career development.

- **Support** –you will most likely face many ups and downs on your journey. Having a strong network will provide you with a support system that you can lean on because they have been where you've been, and they know how to help.

- **Resources** – for every person you add to your network, the power of it grows exponentially based on that person's network. One of the major benefits of having a large network is that you can turn to them for knowledge. If they're unable to help, I'm sure they know someone who can.

"Okay, I got it. A strong professional network is important but how do I go about building one?"

Well, I'm glad you asked. There are many ways to build your network but I'm going to list my favorite below. My recommendation is to try them all and see what works best for you.

- Linkedin
- Meetup
- Events such as conferences, networking events, and hackathons
- Groups/associations at work
- Clubs/associations at your college
- Volunteer groups
- Church groups
- Ask people in your current network for any recommendations on people you should get to know

How you build your network isn't as important as who you add to your network. I'm a big fan of quality over quantity meaning I'd rather have a few people who add lots of value than a bunch of people who add very little value.

Generally, I like to look for the following types of people to add to my network:

- People who share similar goals, values, and outlook on life

- People who are one or two steps ahead of me

- People who are exactly where I want to be

- People who I'm one or two steps ahead of

The goal is to have people at different phases of their career. Those who are one or two steps ahead of you can give you actionable steps and insight on how to get to the next level.

People who are where you want to be can advise you on what to do to get to where they are.

Once you start building your network, don't neglect it. Think of your network as a garden. Planting the seeds is just the first step. If you don't continue to water and give it plenty of sunlight, your garden will die.

Your network is no different, and you will have to continually nourish and care for it if you want to maintain it for as long as you can.

Here are some quick tips on how to take care of your network:

1. Ask how you can add value first before asking for help.

2. Check in every few months, even if it's just a simple email saying hello.

3. Feel free to give an update on how things are going for you but don't forget to ask how you can help the other person.

4. If you come across an article or something on the web that can be of value to the other person, send it.

5. If someone is going through a tough time, don't ask how you can help, show it and show up.

6. Make an introduction if you think that person would benefit from it.

7. Try to be timely with your email or message responses. Nothing looks worse than responding to an email from a month ago.

8. Put yourself in the shoes of the other person and think about what you'd like for yourself and then do it for that person.

Lastly, let me leave you with this story on how my network helped me become an entrepreneur. I attended a small event hosted by a successful entrepreneur named Andrew Warner.

The event was called Scotch night, and a group of about six people got together for drinks with Andrew where we talked about various things. Everyone took turns sharing a personal story about something they were going through at the time.

When it was my turn, I shared how I hated my job and wanted to quit to start my own business. The only problem I had was that I didn't have a business idea. I talked about how my family and friends were disapproving of my decision.

They called me foolish, stupid, and naïve to quit a well-paying job to chase a pipe dream. This affected my self-confidence as it created more self-limiting beliefs for myself.

That night as we left the event, there were two gentlemen who had given me some advice on taking the leap and become an entrepreneur. Before they got into their Uber, one of the gentlemen turned to me and said,

"Hung, if the worst thing that could happen is you try and fail and go back and get a well-paying Silicon Valley job. How bad is it really?"

That single piece of advice changed my outlook. When it was presented that way, it made the decision to quit my job that much easier. That was the power of my network helping me pursue my dreams.

Step 9: Learn to Accept Failure

If there's one advice I could give my dad about parenting, it's that he should have told me it was okay to fail when I was young. In fact, I needed to fail in order to be successful.

Why is that? Well, let me share a bit of family history with you.

Our family of six emigrated from Vietnam to the US in 1980. This was right after the Vietnam War when the communist took over. My parents left everything behind to give my siblings and I a better future.

It took my parents three tries escaping by boat before they were successful. The first time they tried, the boat left them behind because it was full. The second time they got caught, and my dad was thrown in jail for several months.

Then on the third try, they were successful. Although they finally got on the boat, it was far from a sure thing. They still had to deal with dangerous ocean storms, lack of food and water, and sea pirates.

There was no guarantee that they survive the trip. They were at sea for 40 days before they landed in the Philippines. During those 40 days, many people died from sickness and starvation.

Even till this day, they won't say much about what happened. It brings back too many tough memories. It was the ultimate sacrifice for my parents.

Growing up my dad pushed me hard academically to the point where I feared getting a B. He considered that a failure.

Most parents would be happy if their children got those grades but not my dad.

He would accept nothing less than straight A's.

His high expectations drove me nuts. I never felt that anything I did was good enough. This eventually caused a rift between us that lasted for almost 20 years.

Looking back, I can now understand why he was the way he was. When my parents tried to escape Vietnam, failure was not an option. Failure meant a lifetime of suffering for us and possibly death for my dad.

Because of the sacrifices that he made to bring us here, my dad was determined to make sure I made the most out of every opportunity I was given. But in doing so, he destroyed the relationship we had as father and son during high school, college, and most of my adult life.

If there's one thing I learned at a young age, it is that failure is a part of life. Everyone experiences failure. Didn't get that job you wanted? That's a failure. Your relationship didn't work out? That's also a failure.

It's natural to fail. The only thing that matters is how you respond to failure. Are you going to let it keep you down? Or are you going to use it as fuel to feed your fire?

When my parents failed to flee Vietnam the first two times, they could've given up but they didn't. When my dad was sent to prison, he could've said, *"that's enough, I can't risk it anymore,"* but he didn't.

Their dream was to provide us with a better life and a brighter future. It was that dream that kept them going. That dream pushed them through the toughest obstacles until they succeeded.

They never gave up.

That's why it's okay to fail. The sooner you accept that failure is a part of life, the sooner you'll be on your way to success.

Like the famous Japanese saying:

"Fall down seven times, stand up eight."

Fear is one of the world's greatest motivator. The fear of failing and disappointing my dad was what pushed me throughout my adolescence. However, it was inevitable that I would eventually experience failure. My dad refused to see it that way.

The biggest problem for me when I finally failed, was that I didn't know how to respond. I didn't know how to stand back up. I wasn't used to failing. Because I couldn't accept it, I kept feeling that I wasn't good enough. It took me several years before I became okay with failing.

Rather than trying to avoid failure, my advice to you is to learn to accept it. If you can, embrace failure. Look at what hasn't worked and see what you can learn from it.

When failure comes knocking, give it a high five, turn it around, and give it a swift kick in the butt!

"So long failure, it was nice knowing ya!"

When you learn to accept failure, you prepare for it. You accept that things are going to suck for a bit, but you also start working on your resurgence. You already know that you're going to stand up.

There were countless times I didn't get a job offer I wanted. It usually came down to me and another candidate. For whatever reason, the other person always edged me out. I hated that feeling! It got to a point where I stopped interviewing because I couldn't handle being rejected again.

But then I found myself hating my current job even more. I wanted a better job, but because I was tired of being rejected, I stopped trying. How could I expect my situation to change if I stopped trying? Bottom line was, I couldn't.

Do you see the logic here?

So I forced myself to stand up and get back out there. For every rejection that occurred, instead of feeling sorry for myself, I dissected what went wrong. I tried to learn from each experience so that I could improve for next time. I kept pushing harder and harder.

I stopped being afraid and learned to accept failure.

On this personal journey, you're taking, be prepared for setbacks, rejection, and failure. That's just how life works. But remember, the sooner you learn to accept failure, the sooner you can find success.

Step 10: Try Something New Every Month

It's not rocket science, but you'd be surprised at how much better your life would be when you apply this one simple trick.

Try something new every month.

I'm always thinking of ways to level myself up. Sometimes the things I try are pretty drastic but most of the time I work on small improvements.

If there's a new restaurant in town, I'll take a chance on it.

If there's a new workout I haven't done before, I'll give it a try.

If I'm arguing with my wife, I'll take a different approach to resolving it.

I'm sure you see what I'm getting at. You determine what your "something new" is every month. It could be simple, or it could be complex.

For me, trying a new restaurant is simple and doesn't require much effort. On the other hand, taking a different approach to resolving an argument can be more complex.

The goal here is to get in the habit of expanding your horizons. You never know when you will find that one thing or set of things that take your life to the next level.

Here's an example from my personal life. None of my friends are entrepreneurial, and because of this, whenever I had business ideas, it was hard talking to them about it.

They either didn't care or didn't give me productive feedback to help me figure out what to do next. In 2012, I started going to more professional networking events to meet people like myself.

If you know me, I'm a pretty reserved person; some people might even call me shy. Going to mixers and meeting strangers was a big change for me. But I needed to try something new or else my situation wouldn't change.

I met a gentleman by the name of Patrick King. If you look up his name on Amazon, he is the #1 best-selling author on conversation tactics and social confidence. I believe he has about 50 books written, but it could be more.

When I first met Patrick, he had recently left his job as a lawyer to write books. I thought that was fascinating because being a lawyer is thought of as a prestigious career. It's impossible to fathom anyone walking away from a six-figure job to write books.

But Patrick did it. He probably had about five books published at the time and wasn't making much money. However, he shared with me that it wasn't about the money. He hated being a lawyer and wanted a way out.

Writing books started as a hobby. When he saw the opportunity to make money from it, he took the chance and doubled down. Today, his books bring in five figure monthly salaries and have opened so many other business opportunities for him.

Why does this matter?

Well, I wouldn't have written this book if I didn't go to that event and meet Patrick King. Patrick showed me the ropes on how to write and self-publish on Amazon. With his guidance, I've been able to publish several books and help people like yourself in the process.

Sometimes it's funny to think that an opportunity like this can happen from a small chance encounter, but it does happen. If you don't put yourself out there, you won't know when an opportunity might appear that will change your life.

I want you to picture this. There's a basketball hoop, and you are standing in front of it. Next to you, is Michael Jordan, the greatest basketball player to have ever played the game.

You both have the ball in your hands.

You take a shot at the hoop and you miss. Michael, on the contrary, doesn't shoot. Who has the better chance of making the shot? You or Michael Jordan?

Take a wild guess.

If you guessed you, then you're absolutely right. You have a better chance at making that shot than the greatest basketball player ever. And do you know why?

Because you took that shot. Even if you missed, you still have a better chance because you tried. Although Michael Jordan is the greatest basketball player ever, if he doesn't try, then his chances of making the shot is zero.

That's the difference between living the life you want and living the life you settled for.

Take a chance on something new each month and try.

Step 11: Leadership Chooses You

Everybody is capable of leadership because we are all leaders in some form or another. When you make the commitment to unlocking your success, you don't choose to be a leader. Leadership chooses you.

Let me elaborate on that some more.

I use to think that only Type A personalities were leaders. They were outgoing, vocal, and lit every room they walked into. I admired them from a far mainly at how they worked a crowd.

They made it easy to be likeable.

Being an introvert by nature, being a leader didn't come naturally to me. I wasn't born with leadership abilities and thought it was a skill I had to learn and develop. I didn't think I wasn't capable of being a leader.

Boy was I wrong.

Every one of us has leadership abilities; it just takes the right environment to bring it out. In high school, I was one of the quiet kids. While my grades were good, I was told that I had to be well rounded in order to make my college application stand out.

Translation?

I needed to do more to show who I was beside a bookworm. This meant joining student government, a club, and participating in sports. If there was a social group that would allow me to show my leadership abilities, I had to be involved.

So that's what I did, I joined clubs and tried out for the wrestling team. I wasn't an officer in any of the clubs but I found ways to contribute that made me recognized. I wasn't one of the best wrestlers on my team but still practiced hard every day and my teammates saw that.

Slowly my peers started seeing me in a different light. Amongst the quiet kids, I was seen as the outgoing social butterfly.

For lack of a better word, I was the cool nerd.

Because of my strong grades, I received recognition and awards for being a scholar athlete. My teammates on the wrestling team respected me more because the coaches made it known how important grades were to athletics.

They would come to me and ask for help with homework. I started tutoring some of them after practice, and it made me feel good that I could help. When I first joined the team, I was seen as the fragile nerd but by the end of the season, I was one of the captains.

I didn't know it yet, but I was becoming a leader amongst my peers. I didn't set out to become a leader; instead, leadership chose me. As I got older, I took the same approach in college and my professional life. I never forced myself to be a leader. I found opportunities where in the right context, it came naturally.

As you work towards finding your success, you'll come to realize that what you're doing will separate you from your peers. People who strive to get to where you're going will gravitate towards you. Those who want to be who you are will rally to your cause.

They will look to you for motivation because you will be their leader. Whether you chose to be a leader or not, it isn't always your choice. The choice can belong to the people who believe in you and become inspired by you.

That's how you know when leadership chooses you.

And when it happens, don't shy away from it. Don't let the pressure of leading others get to you. Learn to embrace it, and if you fail, it's okay because the people around you will pick you right back up.

Step 12: Going All In

The last and final step is about building a foundation for the future.

Remember, unlocking your true potential and finding success is something that takes time to discover. Finishing this book provides you with a solid framework to start. It's up to you to put in the effort.

Build the mindset of being committed to this quest and work on being better one day at a time. Just like in Texas Hold'em, you've got to go all in.

What does it mean to go all in? Allow me to explain:

- Commit to the steps in this book. Starting new is always easy to do in the beginning, but make an effort to continually apply what you learn over time. This is especially true if you start to get lazy.

- Don't get discouraged when things don't go your way. When it starts to get tough, and you feel disappointed, don't let these things bog you down. Fight through the tough times.

- Don't be afraid to make the tough choices because it's a natural part of your growth. You need to maintain the mindset that short-term sacrifices are meant for long-term benefits.

- You have to believe in everything you're doing without a shadow of a doubt. The minute you start doubting yourself and questioning the choices you make, you take the risk of losing momentum.

- Remove all negative distractions and bad habits from your life. If it's not adding value to your future goals, get rid of it. You need to develop laser-like focus.

- Own who you are. There's nothing to be ashamed of in being different from the crowd. If people laugh at you for being different, laugh at them back for being like everyone else.

- Always keep the big picture in mind. Sometimes I get so bogged down in the day-to-day grind that I lose sight of where I'm going. Take some time and reflect on your progress. Make sure your daily routine aligns with the bigger picture.

- Lastly, have fun. While it is important to be focused and driven, don't forget to take a break now and then and recharge your batteries. What I've found in my experience is that most of the learning and growth comes from the journey and not so much the destination.

People say you can't lose what you don't bet. But I say you can't win if you never take any chances. If you're committed to doing this, then commit yourself to going all the way.

Break Through Success Story #1

Take a guess and see if you can figure out who this is.

At the age of five, his father died.

At the age of 16, he quit school.

At the age of 17, he had already lost four jobs.

At the age of 18, he got married.

Between the ages of 18 and 22, he was a railroad conductor.

At the age of 19, he became a father.

At the age of 20 his wife left him and took their baby daughter.

He joined the army but couldn't cut it.

He applied for law school and was rejected.

He became an insurance salesman and failed again.

Then he became a cook and a dishwasher in a small café.

At the age of 65 he retired.

On the first day of retirement, he received a check from the government for $105.

It made him feel like he wasn't capable of providing for himself.

He thought about suicide because life wasn't worth living anymore; he felt like such a failure.

He sat under a tree and started writing his will. But instead, he wrote what he would have accomplished with his life.

It was then that he realized there was so much more that he hadn't done.

He knew that there was one thing he could do better than anyone else.

And that was how to cook.

So he borrowed $87 and bought ingredients to fry up some chicken using his recipe.

After frying the chicken, he went door to door to sell them to his neighbors in Kentucky.

Remember at age 65, he thought about committing suicide.

But at age 88, he had built an empire and become a millionaire.

This man is Colonel Sanders, and he is the founder of KFC.

Now KFC is the second largest restaurant chain in the world with almost 20,000 locations worldwide in 123 countries.

This is one of my favorite inspirational stories of all time. Colonel Sanders endured many failures and challenges early on in his life. At one point, he even thought about taking his own life, but he didn't.

Instead, he gave it one last try. He set out on an adventure that would ultimately turn his life around and cement his legacy. If there's one thing I want you to take away from his story, it's that you're never too old to dream and achieve success.

You've dealt with hardships before, and chances are, you have a few more to overcome before you break through. But when things are tough and you feel like giving up. Remember this story and how Colonel Sanders didn't find success until well past this 60's.

Remember his grit, his persistence, and his courage.

Keep fighting and moving forward.

Break Through Success Story #2

I have one more success story for you. See if you can guess who this is.

He was born into poverty.

At a young age, his family was forced out of their home, and he had to work to support them.

His mom died when he was only nine years old.

He failed numerous times in business.

He ran for state legislature and lost.

He lost his job and applied for law school but was denied.

He borrowed money to start a business that went bankrupt. He spent the next 17 years paying off his debt.

He ran for state legislature again and won.

He was engaged to be married, but his sweetheart died before they could marry. He was extremely heart broken.

He had a nervous breakdown and was in bed for six months.

He ran for speaker of the state legislature and lost.

He ran for Congress and lost.

He ran for Congress a second time and won, but when he ran for re-election to Congress, he lost.

He ran for the US Senate and lost.

He ran for the US Senate again and lost.

He was elected President of the United States.

This man was Abraham Lincoln, the sixteenth president of the United States.

We rarely find examples of constant persistence for success, like those of Abraham Lincoln. Like Colonel Sanders, Abraham Lincoln didn't find success until much later in life. His early life was marred by many bouts of failure and rejection.

He could have quit many times, but he didn't and became one of the greatest presidents in America.

Bonus Step: If Nothing is Going Right, Do This One Trick

You wake up, grab your phone, and realize it's 9am. Your alarm didn't go off, and you're late for work. On most days this wouldn't be that big of an issue, but not today. Today, you are presenting in front of a group of senior executives.

You rush to get ready, skip breakfast, and jump in the car. You can still make it to work, except now your gas tank is on empty. You call for an Uber, get to the office, rush inside only to discover you left your presentation on a USB stick at home.

Needless to say, everything that could go wrong did go wrong.

I know this story very well because this happened to me once.

Now as a one-time incident, it's easy to forget it and move on. But what if it wasn't a one-time incident? What if your life felt like this every day? How can you hold on until you get your big break?

Easy, with this one simple trick.

Do something good for someone. That's it; it's that simple.

When we do good deeds for others, our brain releases endorphins which are chemicals that give us feelings of euphoria. Similar to the high one can get from running, doing something good for others makes us feel good about ourselves.

Our brain also gets a serotonin boost which has been linked to feelings of satisfaction and self-confidence. As we feel good about ourselves, guess what also happens? Our stress levels go down which is a boost to our overall health.

If you're struggling to figure out what to do, here are ten easy suggestions:

1. Take someone out to lunch
2. Surprise your significant other with flowers
3. Call a friend who you haven't talked to in a while and make plans to catch up
4. Offer to mentor somebody in your company
5. Help a child with his or her homework
6. Cook dinner for your parents
7. Bring your co-workers donuts
8. Buy and mail a friend their favorite book
9. If you're grabbing coffee, buy the person behind you a cup of coffee
10. Record a video message thanking a friend and send it to him or her

Again, these don't require much effort to do and the benefit is great for your overall well-being. There's no time to stress when you're feeling good about yourself.

Conclusion

You did it!

You made it through the 12 critical steps in building grit, destroying negativity, and developing the resilience to achieve long term goals. While you may not see it yet, following the instructions in this book will help you make huge improvements in your personal and career development.

Self-limiting beliefs are tough to deal with. We've all battled periods of self-doubt and low self-esteem. While nobody is immune to them, the good news is that they aren't permanent.

If you ever feel stuck or unsure about your direction, read this book again. You will find that each time you read it; you'll gain a different perspective and understanding on how to approach life.

We're all capable and deserving of being the best we can be. Don't ever think for a minute that you're relegated to the life you have. You have a right to stake your claim in this world.

And last but not least, if Colonel Sanders can rebuild his life and be a millionaire well past his sixties, so can you.

Make it yours and own it!

Sincerely,

Hung Pham

If you enjoyed this book and want more tips and strategies on building a better life, sign up for my newsletter at: http://www.missionandpossible.com

P.S. If you found this book valuable, could you please take a minute and leave a review for this book on Amazon? Your feedback will help me continue to write Kindle books that produce positive results in your life.

P.S.S. If you enjoyed this book, I highly recommend you check out my other Amazon bestseller books on <u>personal development here</u>.

Cheat Sheet

Step 1: Your self-beliefs come from what you believe to be true about yourself.

Step 2: Your self-limiting beliefs usually come from an external source or experience that influences how you think.

Step 3: Challenge your self-limiting beliefs by using one of these three strategies: role play, write it down, or reverse your thinking.

Step 4: To find your voice, block out distractions. Figure out what your epic quest is and how you plan on changing the world.

Step 5: Everyone has an inner critic that wants them to fail. Challenge your inner critic with every win until it has nothing else to say but silence.

Step 6: Study the successful people who you aspire to be like in this world. Figure out what their routine and habits are and make it a part of your life.

Step 7: Start creating your digital footprint. Put yourself out there and own it. Be proud of who you are even if you think you don't have much to show yet.

Step 8: Treat your network like a carefully cultivated garden. You need to nourish it, in order for it to grow and let you reap the benefits.

Step 9: Failure is a part of the life. The sooner you can accept it, the sooner you can get back on your horse and ride again.

Step 10: Try new things at least once a month to broaden your horizons. You never know when that one thing helps you level up.

Step 11: When people come to your side because you inspire them, embrace it and allow yourself to be a leader.

Step 12: Commit to building a successful life for the long run. Don't leave yourself any outs, go all in.

Bonus Step: When nothing seems to be going right, do a good deed for someone else.

About the Author

Hung Pham is the founder of <u>Culture Summit</u>, a conference that helps companies succeed through building strong cultures. Before Culture Summit,

Hung spent over ten years working at several Fortune 100 companies.

In his 20s, Hung dealt with a serious gambling addiction that led to severe depression and financial debt. Through hard work and persistence, he has turned his life around and become a successful entrepreneur. You can learn how too by downloading his free 33-page eBook at www.missionandpossible.com.

Printed by Amazon Italia Logistica S.r.l.
Torrazza Piemonte (TO), Italy

13744123R10059

Billionaire Daddy Series

Ex-Military Billionaire Daddy (Book 3)

S.E. Riley

The Redherring Publishing House

Ex-Military
Billionaire Daddy
(Book 3)

Table of Contents

Prologue

Maddie Hayes surveyed the lavish spread of food on the table. When Liam had asked her to come over for dinner with her three-year old son Trystam, he'd asked what she wanted to eat. She'd told him she missed the luxury of a good steak and potatoes, but she hadn't expected this. The cook had prepared fresh, made-from-scratch mashed potatoes, perfectly seared steak garnished with parsley and lemon, steamed vegetables, and crème brûlée for dessert.

"Is everything all right, Mad?" Liam's sister Jessica settled a moderate portion of steak and potatoes on her plate before passing the dish to Liam. "You're staring at your plate of food like you can't quite believe what you're seeing."

Maddie looked up from the plate, heat flushing her cheeks. "Oh...everything is fine. More than fine." She met Liam's attentive gaze and cleared her throat, shifting in her seat. "It's more than I imagined when Liam asked me what I wanted for dinner."

Jessica laughed. "You know my brother doesn't do things halfway, Maddie. Of course he'd make sure dinner was spectacular."

Liam smiled indulgently. "I had to do something special to convince you to come back. Good food seems to be the only way I can coax a visit from you these days, and with my busy schedule at the security firm, I can't exactly drop in whenever unannounced. I'm glad you could make it."

She smiled back and dropped her gaze to the plate of food in front of her. Liam had done so much for her. She couldn't quite believe he still wanted her around after all he'd seen her through. Trystam's father leaving for a job opportunity in another state while she was a few months pregnant had devastated her, made worse by him saying a child would only slow him down. But Liam—who had just returned from a long, difficult tour in Iraq—had stepped in to help as soon as he heard what had happened.

He'd been starting up the security firm in those days, barely a year into operating it, yet he'd often spare time from his schedule to look after her.

He'd show up to check that she'd had lunch and taken her vitamins, staying over to keep an eye on her in the early days when she was sick often. And he'd taken her to the hospital when labor hit.

He'd been there even though she'd wished the man who'd put her in this position was instead, and he hadn't once complained about her late-night rants or the emotions that followed as she struggled to move past her ex.

Liam had been furious with her, offering to drag her ex back and set him straight, but she'd refused to give him her ex's details, including his name.

Even after all that, he still made time for her and wanted to see her and Trystam. She glanced at the baby monitor on the sideboard across the room and cut into her steak.

"Don't worry about him, Maddie," Liam murmured. "You're here to take a break. He's sleeping in my room, and he's fine. He's getting big now, and he can handle getting up and calling for us if he needs you."

She nodded and released a slow breath before digging into her food with enthusiasm. She hadn't had a good meal like this in a long time, and she certainly hadn't been eating anything close to it in the last few months. She and Trystam had been surviving off macaroni and cheese, peanut butter, and toast. Sometimes she managed a little chicken, but things were tight right now, and she rarely had the money to afford it.

"So, how are things at the vet?" Jessica asked before taking a bite of her vegetables.

Maddie swallowed the bite she'd taken, her appetite ebbing. "Oh...they're...fine, I guess."

Liam's eyes narrowed, his usual response when she lied to him. He hated it when she kept secrets and told half-truths or outright lies. I

f she'd been his to care for, she expected he'd have taken her to task for it more openly and sternly, but the expression on his face perfectly conveyed his irritation and disappointment, anyway.

"Maddie," he murmured in a warning tone. "Just fine?"

She shifted in her seat and swallowed hard. "All right...they closed a few months ago."

"Oh..." Jessica frowned. "Well, have you been able to pick up more hours at the diner?"

"I've tried. They don't have the hours for me."

Liam scowled. "So what have you been doing to pay bills and put food on the table, missy?"

"What is this? The Spanish Inquisition?"

"You'd know if it were an inquisition," Liam drawled. "Right now, I'm just asking."

Jessica stifled a smile. Maddie shot her a glare. So much for sisterly solidarity from her best friend.

"I'm waiting." Liam set down his silverware. "Maddie?"

"All right, all right." She heaved a sigh. "I haven't found anything to make up for losing the secretarial position at the vet."

"But what are you eating, and how do you pay bills on the pay from the diner?"

Maddie flushed and stared down at her plate.

"Maddie Hayes," Liam rumbled. "You should have said something. You know I'd have helped."

Her cheeks warmed further. "You shouldn't have to bail me out all the time."

"I'm not." Liam sat back and crossed his arms. "I have a position open for a secretary, and I haven't been able to fill it yet. If you'd told me months ago, I would've offered you the job right at the beginning."

She bit her lower lip. "Liam, I can't...I won't take a job just because—"

"Don't you dare finish that sentence, missy." Liam glanced over at Jessica. "Jessica, I'll understand if you don't want to sit through this conversation. I can go discuss this with Maddie in the library."

"No," Maddie snapped. "I'm not a wayward child to be taken into hand, Liam. I don't want handouts, either."

"It isn't a handout," Jessica murmured with a bemused smile. "Not when Liam's offering the job. He'll demand his money's worth out of you just like he does any other employee."

Maddie's annoyance ebbed a bit. Jessica was right about that much. Liam didn't accept half measures any more than he offered them.

"I want you in my office at eight tomorrow morning," Liam told her. "I need a secretary, and you need a job, Maddie. The only answer I want to hear from you is 'yes, sir'. Understood?"

The blush returned with a vengeance. "All right."

He pinned her with an impatient stare, one brow lifting in expectation.

"Yes, sir," she mumbled.

Liam nodded, and the other two returned to their meals. She followed suit shortly after, wishing she didn't feel so embarrassed by her situation. She'd hoped to have a solution *before* Liam discovered she'd kept her financial difficulties from him so that it could remain her secret. He'd done so much for her already.

Sighing, she consoled herself with the reminder that this would be a job. He wasn't handing her the paycheck; she'd have to earn it, and every cent of that check every two weeks would be hers, fair and square.

He was helping out, but he wasn't taking her independence from her or asking her to rely on him for everything.

For that, she was grateful.

Chapter 1

Two years later

Liam Beckett climbed out of his Maserati and headed into the building that housed his private security firm. He opened the door and nodded to the receptionist at the front door, who smiled back with a quiet greeting. He made his way up to the top floor where his offices were located and found Maddie waiting at her desk with his coffee and hers in a cardboard drink holder on her desk's neat surface.

"Maddie," he murmured.

"Liam." She looked up from her work and grinned, snatching his coffee from the drink holder and handing it over. "I've finalized your meetings. Unless anyone stops by unannounced and without an appointment, you have a light load for meetings today."

He took the coffee from her, his fingers lingering on hers a little longer than strictly necessary. She caught the lingering touch and looked away, withdrawing her hand quickly.

A frown furrowed his brow before he could stop his reaction.

A cute, delicate blush brought color to his cheeks and soothed the sting her haste to pull back had caused. He smiled at her again and moved past her toward the office door behind her desk. "How is Trystam doing?"

He leaned against the doorframe and sipped his coffee, watching her face for any signs of distress or trouble.

She gave him a broad smile. "He's doing well. All over the sniffles from his cold, and he's chattering incessantly about your promise to take him to the science museum."

Liam laughed. "That boy loves science more than any kid I've ever known. Like mother, like son, in this case."

She shifted and stared down at her keyboard. "What's wrong with liking science? I know it might be nerdy, but he'll make good money if he chooses to pursue the interest into a career."

Liam pushed away from the door and walked back to the desk, setting the coffee down on the desk and crouching in front of her. "Hey, I wasn't making light of it. There's nothing wrong with it at all, Mad."

She bit her lower lip and stared down at him. "You mean that?"

"I do. You know me well enough to know I wouldn't tease or make fun of you or Trystam for it, missy. Why the defensiveness?"

She sighed and relaxed. "I'm sorry. I just...old habits die hard."

"Yes, I can see that. This is what? The hundredth time I've had to tell you there's nothing to be embarrassed about?"

"In my defense, I've been teased and given a hard time about being the...nerd since I was a schoolgirl. People at work think I'm odd for being so interested in it still at 27, and...and..."

"And he used to mock you for it, didn't he?" Liam clenched his jaw and looked away, furious to learn of yet another way the man who had abandoned her after knocking her up had left scars. "You know, I'm still happy to track this jerk down and make a point."

A tiny laugh escaped her. "It's a little late for that, Liam. Leave it alone. And thank you for reminding me that at least one person doesn't think I'm crazy, nerdy, or weird."

"Well...I think you're nerdy," he murmured, reaching up to brush her hair from her face. "I just happen to think it's cute rather than weird."

The blush returned, and she didn't respond to the remark.

He stood and retrieved his coffee. "Someday, you'll stop bristling when I make comments about this. It might take more time, but I'll find a way."

She snorted. "Liam, it's been what? Five years...it's a habit."

"A habit you can unlearn. Don't you trust me?"

The look on her face was torn. So she still feared what might happen if she trusted him, but at the same time, her experience told her he could be trusted.

Maddie was too independent and stubborn to just let him take care of things, to trust him to take charge and not run out like her ex had. The man had left deep scars, and even though Liam had stuck around and made it clear he intended to keep doing so, she still looked at him like she was afraid he'd leave at any moment when he finally understood the kind of person she was.

He knew full well who Maddie Hayes was, though, and he had zero intention of walking away.

It would just take time to show her that he wasn't helping out of some sense of duty to his sister or even to her and Trystam but because he genuinely cared and wanted to be there.

He was in this for the long game.

He wanted her, and he loved her son like his own. There was no way he'd give that up, even if she never chose to see him as he'd come to see her.

"Let me know when the first appointment arrives, and make sure you take your lunch today, Maddie. I don't want to see you eating over your work when I take my own lunch break, understood?"

"Yes, sir."

He smiled at her once more and then spun on his heel and headed for the office before he let her know just how much he liked it when she was sweet and obedient instead of stubborn and mulish. She wasn't ready yet.

He needed to ease her into the idea of going beyond friendship, not toss her off the deep end. He'd find a way to do this slow and right so he wouldn't send her running for the hills.

***

Liam's phone rang, cutting through the quiet in his office. The outer office was empty. Maddie had taken the afternoon off to attend a parent-teacher day at Trystam's school, and the receptionist at the front desk had been handling his meetings and calls. He answered it absentmindedly. "Yes?"

"Your next appointment is here to see you, Mr. Beckett. Mr. Alyx Marlin?"

"Send him up, then." Liam pulled up his email and glanced over the email Marlin had sent. The man was a high-powered district attorney dealing with a gang-related issue and wanted extra security to protect him from a slew of threats and a few assassination attempts.

There was a knock at the door.

"Come in."

His floor's receptionist entered along with a thin, nervous looking man with eyes that couldn't remain fixed on one place for long.

"Mr. Marlin, sir," his receptionist said.

"Thank you, Bessie."

The receptionist left the room. He ushered Marlin to a seat, immediately disliking the man. His personal unease and dislike for a client didn't matter, though. Marlin could pay well, and although the man wasn't the DA for their little part of the state and held no sway here, it didn't hurt to have friends in high places. "Tell me about the situation, Mr. Marlin."

The man rubbed his hands together with a grimace. "I've been dealing with the organized crime case going on in Minneapolis. I told you in my email I've received death threats and had attempts made on my life. My own security detail hasn't really stopped the issue, so I want extra outside help."

"Do you believe your own security detail is compromised?"

"I suspect so, but I can't prove it, and proving it is everything."

The man smiled wanly. "I've barely been able to sleep for fear they'll try again, whoever they are. I want them handled and my life safe and stable again."

"You've come to the right place for security. We'll need to discuss further details, though. You need to keep a closer eye on the security team you already have, and I'll be reviewing any footage from your security system that might help. How many members of the team do you already have?"

"Three. I have an armed escort whenever I need to go somewhere, but those are the three who handle security for me and my home twenty-four-seven."

"I see. All vetted carefully?"

"Of course." The man straightened his jacket. "What do you take me for? A fool?"

Perhaps if you imagine safety and stability were possible in a DA's position, Liam mused.

"I'd like to see the background checks, and I need a list of everyone who has a key or access to your home and personal office. The first two attacks happened in your home, correct? Bombs, if I recall?"

Marlin paled as the attacks were brought up in more detail, but he nodded. "You've done your research."

"What do you take me for?" Liam smiled, though the smile was more teeth than it was a friendly gesture. "A fool? You came to me for a reason, Mr. Marlin. It was because I am the best, not just here but in several states, and my firm is renowned for its excellence across the country."

"I didn't mean any insult by it."

"It's not as though the details were difficult to find," Liam murmured. "I will assign two of my men to escort you. I think it would be best if you stayed in a safe house until we can sort out this issue."

"I won't be kept from going about errands and daily life by these thugs, Mr. Beckett."

"I don't expect that, for now, but I want you in a place I control until we know the threat is past. I cannot afford to try to protect you from your own men in a place where they have a home court advantage, if one of them is indeed involved. These thugs have proven resourceful enough to find their way into your home despite your security. Clearly, that location is not safe."

Marlin grimaced and nodded, but he pressed his lips together in a tight white line, looking ready to explode in frustration.

"I won't fight with you over your safety, Mr. Marlin. If you don't like how I'm handling the situation, then find another firm that will handle it more to your liking. I don't take clients who argue with me. It only increases the risk of harm or death if I do, both for them and for my men."

"Understood," Marlin muttered. "I'll pack a bag. Where is this safe house?"

"My men will take you there. You will bring no one from your original security team. Tell them you want them to continue patrolling your home to make it appear as though you are still there. That will keep them where I can easily find and question them if necessary, and it will also increase the chances that we catch whoever is responsible from trying again."

"You want me to have my security team house sit?" Marlin gaped at him. "On their salary?"

Liam folded his hands in front of him on the desk and stared at Marlin without a word. Either the man understood the danger he was facing or didn't.

If he didn't, Liam would cut him loose.

He either agreed to the request now, or he was going to the curb and would have to find someone else.

Marlin swallowed hard. "Fine. When will your men arrive?"

"8 AM tomorrow morning. I need time to set up everything for the safe house. I'll have some men watching the estate and the house to make sure you're not harmed in the meantime." He rose, buttoning his jacket and extending a hand to Marlin. "A pleasure to be doing business with you, Mr. Marlin."

Marlin scowled, but he shook Liam's hand anyway before turning stiffly and exiting the room, leaving Liam to himself.

Chapter 2

Liam put the matter of Mr. Marlin out of his mind the next day when Maddie showed up. She looked a little tired, and he frowned as he stopped at her desk for the usual coffee. "What were you up late for?"

She took a sip of her coffee and sighed, leaning back in her office chair. "I was just restless. I couldn't sleep."

"I see. Are you feeling all right? You aren't coming down with anything, are you?"

"No, thank you. Just a case of racing thoughts before bed." She smiled at him warmly.

The smile left a warmth in his gut, and he wanted nothing more than to come straight out and tell her he wanted more from her. Instead, he focused on the plan he'd developed and on moving slowly. "Racing thoughts about what?"

"Oh, this and that," she mumbled.

He raised a brow. "Sounds a bit vague. What's really going on, Mad?"

"Nothing." She glanced up at him, scooted closer to her desk, and began cleaning up the pens she'd left before taking off yesterday. "Really, Liam. I promise."

"All right. Do you have a minute? I wanted to ask you something."

She frowned and looked up from her desk. "About what? You sound a little nervous."

"I am," he admitted. "But I'm hoping for a yes to prove I didn't need to be."

"Okay..." Trepidation tensed the lines of her shoulders. "What's wrong?"

"Nothing. I wanted you to go to dinner with me."

"Oh." She laughed, relaxing. "That's not so bad. Are we meeting a client?"

"No. I don't need you to take notes, and it's not for business."

"Oh, okay. Well, I'm sure Trystam would enjoy dinner out."

"You mistake me, missy." He smiled gently, leaning on the desk with his hip. "I want *you* to go to dinner with me. We'll find Trystam a babysitter."

She flushed. "I...I see. You want to..."

"You work hard enough, Maddie. Let me take you out someplace fun, just like we used to do when we were all kids."

She bit her lower lip, and he forced himself to ignore the building desire to take her face in his hands and kiss her senselessly so that any doubts she had about his intentions would be erased. Instead, he stayed still and waited for an answer.

"But it's just us. Isn't that...kind of like a date?"

"Call it whatever you want," he murmured, noting the indecision and worry on her face. "I didn't want you worried or upset by a request to spend time with a woman I consider a friend."

The worry lifted, but she still didn't seem certain. "When did you want to go? I can't get a sitter on such short notice..."

"We'll figure out the best time, and I'll handle the sitter. I'll ask Mrs. Potts to watch him if we can't find anyone. She won't mind."

"We can't ask your housekeeper, Liam!" She looked appalled. "She has a life outside of working for you, and her job doesn't include watching a little boy who gets into mischief."

"Mrs. Potts likes Trystam, as you well know. I'd pay her for it too, but we'll see if we can find another babysitter."

"What will people think?" she whispered, looking away.

"What will people think?" he echoed, incredulous. "Who cares? Everyone in the office knows we're friends, Maddie. No one will care, and no one will talk, either. They know I have zero tolerance for gossip, especially in a security firm where we have to keep secrets discreetly for clients."

She licked her lips. "It's not our usual behavior."

"Maddie," he murmured.

Her gaze shot to his at the stern tone in his quiet voice.

"Are you making excuses, missy?"

The blush swept up into the delicate shells of her ears, and she lowered her gaze, hiding her pretty brown eyes. "We don't go places one on one. We're not that kind of friend to each other."

"If that's what you think, perhaps I need to try harder. I'd like us to be that kind of friend, Madison Hayes."

Her eyes widened at the use of her full first name. "W-well...if you're sure..."

"I've never been more sure in my life."

"I guess I could go. But where are we going and when? I don't know if I have anything nice enough for a personal...I mean, can one wear the same things to personal dinners as to business ones? How nice is the restaurant? If you maybe pick one—"

He pressed his index finger to her lips with a bemused smile. "Maddie, take a breath. Dress comfortably. Casual is fine. I'm not going to make a spectacle of you by taking you somewhere that makes you feel out of place or small and insignificant. Where we're going is a surprise, though. Trust me?"

She closed her eyes with a soft sigh. "Okay."

"Good girl. How about we go Friday night at six?" He pulled his finger away from her lips. "If we can't find a sitter, I'll pay Mrs. Potts. She's usually free Friday nights."

Her eyes opened, and she stared up at him with a mixture of uncertainty and warmth. "Thank you, Liam."

He smiled. "I'm the one who ought to thank you for agreeing. I thought you might not for a minute there."

She laughed quietly, cheeks pinking again. "I haven't gone out somewhere with a man one-on-one in ages. I'm not even sure I know what to do."

He gave in to his urge to touch her just a little, pressing a chaste kiss to her forehead as he picked up his coffee. "Just be yourself, missy. That's enough, I promise."

Her expression betrayed her disagreement, but she didn't argue the point with him, so he left it be. He headed into his office, leaving her to think about what she'd agreed to and smiling to himself. Step one was accomplished, at least.

Now he just had to figure out ways to hint to her that he was interested in seeing how she felt about the idea. He had a suspicion she liked him by how she reacted to his touch or the commanding note he sometimes injected into his tone, but he wanted to be certain before he risked their friendship for more.

***

She was stunned when Liam parked his Maserati in front of a little pizza place in a more rundown part of town. While they'd all grown up with relatively poor backgrounds—something that had contributed to Liam's decision to join the military—Liam no longer lived in that world. Neither did Jessica. She was the only one who did, to some extent. That Liam not only knew about a hole-in-the-wall place like this but also took her to it was astonishing.

Was this a place he took all his dates? Or was it unique to her because he thought she'd be too overwhelmed if he took her somewhere fancy? He climbed out, oblivious to her anxiety, and opened the car door for her. She let him draw her out and guide her up to the door of the small restaurant.

He opened this door, too, ushering her into the warm, inviting interior of the building. The staff stopped what they were doing to stare. They seemed to know Liam, but judging by the confusion on some of the faces and the outright delight on others, she guessed he must not bring any dates here. She wasn't *really* a date, but from the outside, it probably looked like she was, and they seemed to assume it.

"Mr. Beckett." A short Italian man with a broad smile approached and clasped Liam's hand warmly. "Good to see you. Who is this lovely young lady on your arm?"

She felt the heat of embarrassment creeping into her cheeks and then her ears, and she stared down at the floor.

Liam drew her closer, tucking her into his side. "This is Maddie. We're old friends, and she works with me."

"Ah, I see, I see." The man clapped his hands and rubbed them together. "Would you like the corner booth, Mr. Beckett? It offers more privacy."

"Thank you, Giuliano. That would be wonderful."

Liam guided her to the booth and helped her slide in. Instead of taking a seat across from her as she'd expected, he slid in next to her, keeping his warm thigh pressed against her. She bit her lip and contemplated scooting over more. Did he feel crowded? If he did, though, there was room to move, and he didn't remark on it. He'd sat this close on purpose. Her cheeks warmed. Why was he so close? What game was he playing?

He leaned in closer, whispering in her ear. "Relax, Maddie. We're just out for dinner and a little fun after."

"Why is everyone staring at me like they think I'm...like they think I'm..." *Yours*, was what hovered on the tip of her tongue, but she couldn't make herself voice it.

"I don't bring other people here." He leaned back, taking his warmth with him.

She sighed, missing the warmth even as she questioned her sanity for letting herself imagine the man, who was both her *boss* and one of her closest friends, doing more than merely whispering in her ear. This was insane.

His hand landed on her thigh.

She jumped, gasping.

He raised a brow. "Someone's jumpy. I brought you here because I really like this place, and I thought you might too. I hope you're hungry, though. They make huge pizzas."

Relaxing, she picked up the menu, letting herself indulge in a moment of weakness by leaning against him. Really, if he didn't like it, he had only himself to blame since he was sitting so close. If he did mind, he didn't say anything.

He perused the menu as if she hadn't leaned into him at all. The part of her that enjoyed pushing for a reaction wanted to see how far she could go before he scolded her, but they were in public, and she didn't want to make a spectacle of the teasing banter they shared in private.

"You've gone very quiet over there, missy," he murmured. "Are you asleep or plotting something?"

She coughed and sat up. "N-neither!"

"Mmm...plotting then. What's going through that cute head of yours?"

She ducked her head and avoided his gaze. When he said things like that, it reminded her that he was quite a bit older. Almost eight years divided them, and he wouldn't see her as a woman when he'd been taking care of her like she was his little sister all these years.

His hand returned to her thigh, rubbing in soothing circles over the thin fabric of the floral skirt she'd worn for the outing. "It's all right if you want to keep it a secret. I'm sure I'll have it out of you eventually, if not because you fessed up, then because you put the plan into action. Just know that if you and Trystam switch out my shaving cream for whipped cream again, it's your butt on the line."

She giggled, the tension easing. It was ridiculous to be so stressed about this! It was Liam. He was safe and solid, unlike so much else in her life. He'd never do anything to hurt or upset her intentionally, and however sad she might be that the mixed signals he gave off didn't mean anything, there was no reason to let that sadness stop her from enjoying this time with him.

"That's better." He smiled softly.

The waiter came to take their order, and the rest of the meal went by in easy conversation. His shoulder brushed hers as they ate and hers bumped his every so often. If it bothered him to have her so close, he didn't show any signs of it. When the meal was demolished, he paid the check, refusing to let her touch her wallet or the bill.

Once they'd made it back to the car, she bit her lip and settled into the seat. He buckled her in before she could do it and then rounded the car to climb into the driver's seat.

She smiled shyly when she found his gaze on her. "You said we would have fun after dinner...what did you mean?"

"Well..." He turned the car on, the engine purring to life quietly, and then pulled out onto the road. "It's a surprise, but I promise it'll be a good one. I hope you still like games as much as you did when you were younger."

Games? Of course she did, but what kind of games? She sat on the edge of her seat, trying not to plead with him to give her clues. He smirked when he saw her wiggling, and she stopped immediately, folding her hands in her lap as her cheeks warmed.

"It's cute that you still get so excited about surprises," he murmured, reaching over to pull her hands away from worrying at the fabric of her skirt. They'd been driving for close to ten minutes now.

"I'm not a little kid, you know," she mumbled. "I'm not supposed to be cute."

"Adults can be cute too." He pulled up in front of a large building with a neon *Arcade* sign out front.

A grin spread across her face as she processed where he'd taken her. "An arcade?"

"You used to love them when we were kids."

"You remembered?" she whispered.

"Of course I did, missy."

Tears prickled at the corners of her eyes. "I can't believe you cared enough to remember..."

"Stop that," he commanded sternly. "You know I care, Maddie. Don't put yourself down by insinuating you're not worth my attention or concern."

She flushed, and peeked up at him from underneath her lashes before he walked out. When he rounded the car to help her out this time, she didn't hesitate to take his hand. After all, she was excited to play whatever games the arcade had with Liam, and she didn't want to waste a single second. Not when he was here with her, making the night perfect and stress-free so long as she allowed herself to trust him and to enjoy it.

Chapter 3

Liam's interest in taking her out didn't stop with the trip to the arcade, though his next request included Trystam, much to her relief. As much as she'd enjoyed his attention, one-on-one time with Liam was dangerous. It tempted her to forget that he was just a good friend and one she owed a great deal to, not someone who would ever see her as girlfriend material, let alone more. Besides, there was Trystam to think of, and he would be devastated if something happened between her and Liam to cause the man to stop visiting.

"Mommy, it's a dolphin!" Trystam's squeal of delight brought her back to the present moment with her son and the man whose presence had her daydreaming.

She smiled at her son and Liam, carrying the boy on his broad shoulders as they moved through the giant aquarium. "It is, isn't it?"

"I learned all about dolphins in school this week," the proud five-year-old announced. "Did you know they're really not fish, Mr. Liam?"

Liam tipped his head up to look at the boy with a grave look. "I didn't. What else did you learn?"

"They're mammals," the boy declared. "And they breathe through a hole at the top of their heads. And my teacher says they have emotional capacities that are super close to humans."

"Impressive. What do you think, missy? Impressive?"

She smiled at him and then up at Trystam, who was holding onto Liam's head and watching her anxiously. "I think it's very impressive, Trystam. You learned a lot from class this week, didn't you?"

"I always learn lots in class, Mommy," he said, his attention going back to the dolphins with wide-eyed fascination.

She joined them at the window. "Do you think we could stay and watch them for a while? I know it's probably dull, but he's never seen a dolphin, Liam. Not in real life."

Liam pulled the amazed child from his shoulders and sat him on the bench beside the glass. He took a seat beside the child and pulled her down to sit with them. "I could watch these guys play all day. It's just a bit more fun to watch him watch them like this."

Trystam got up and ran to the glass just in front of the bench as one of the dolphins swam by, chasing after another.

She sighed in quiet contentment. "Thank you, Liam. It's not often he gets to go places this nice. I try to take him to parks and attractions, but...well, it's not really a priority, and it's hard to swing it as a single mom when I have to work. Not that I'm complaining, mind you. I like working, and I like working for you. I just..."

He reached out and took her hand in his, holding it as the two of them watched Trystam. "You just wish you had the luxury of spending this time with him while he's still young enough to be like this."

She bit her lower lip and stared down at their entwined hands. "Yeah."

"That might be possible in the future, Maddie."

"Not likely. Who wants to date, let alone marry, a woman bringing a kid along with her?"

"Well, I don't consider that a deal breaker. Trystam's a great kid, and any man should be proud if he gets the chance to be that little boy's father figure."

She felt her cheeks warm and looked away. He was just saying that because he'd known Trystam since the boy was a baby. "You're just being nice. It's easy to say it's not a deal breaker when you're talking about a kid you know. Trystam's a good kid, but most men won't care about that. They'll see him as a commitment they don't want to take on in addition to me."

His glare settled heavy on her, and she could sense his displeasure without even looking. His fingers tightened on hers when she tried to pull away. "Then you're not talking about men, sweetheart. You're talking about boys. Men don't hide from commitment."

Men like Liam didn't hide from commitment. Plenty of others did. "I still think you're just being nice. A significant other isn't in the cards for me. Even if I didn't have Trystam, I'm a little too—"

A sharp tug on the end of her ponytail grabbed her attention and drew her gaze to his. He frowned at her sternly. "You'd better not have been about to put yourself down, little girl. I don't take kindly to that, and if I have to start doing something about it, I will. Maybe we need our own version of a swear jar to put a stop to it."

She huffed. "I wasn't going to say anything that isn't true," she muttered.

He opened his mouth to reply, but Trystam returned, a big smile on his face, and put a stop to the conversation. "Mommy, can we go see the sharks too? My teacher taught me about them too."

She stood a little too quickly, pulling her hand out of Liam's sharply. Trystam's gaze wandered first to Liam and then to her, but the child didn't seem upset by the hand-holding. Usually, Liam didn't touch her in front of him. He kept his hands strictly to himself, in general, most of the time. This time had been a rare moment of public affection from her friend. Would Trystam be confused? He viewed Liam as a father, but he knew that Liam wasn't anything more than a friend, just like he knew he had a biological dad out there somewhere.

"Mommy, it's not nice to pull your hand out of someone else's. You always tell me I can't let go of yours in places like this." He pointed at Liam, who was smiling broadly. "He just wants to make sure you don't get lost, just like you always do with me."

She closed her eyes and fought back a laugh. Trystam came up with the strangest reasoning for things at times.

"Yeah, Maddie," Liam teased. "We wouldn't want to lose you, so hand in mine, missy."

She opened her eyes and sighed, extending her hand to him. When Trystam was safely holding Liam's other hand, she cast her friend an annoyed look and mouthed 'jerk'.

He smirked back and shook his head, leaning in to murmur, "The kid had a valid point, Maddie."

"He did not," she hissed back. "What's with the excuse to hold my hand, anyway? Are you just trying to get under my skin?"

His smile was too innocent. "That's for me to know and you to find out. Now, I believe a certain someone asked about the sharks."

Trystam was tugging at Liam's hand, urging him to move faster. "I saw the sign for the sharks up there!" He pointed, almost skipping in his haste to get to the next exhibit.

"They'll still be there in another five or ten minutes, kiddo," Liam chided gently. "Slow down and enjoy everything along the way. Did you see these colorful fish over here? I bet your teacher hasn't taught you about angel fish yet."

Attention successfully diverted, Trystam hurried over to the display Liam was guiding him to without protest. He stared in at the brightly colored fish with wide eyes. "They're so pretty. Did someone paint them those colors?"

Liam bent down to the boy's level, releasing Maddie's hand to point at the fish. "Nope, they're this way naturally. Isn't that cool?"

"Why are they like that naturally?" her son wondered.

S.E. Riley

"Because they swim around in the corals and need to blend in. See?" He pointed at the coral below.

"So it's like camouflage?" the boy asked.

"Just like camouflage."

Maddie watched the two of them discuss the fish with a pang of sorrow. What would it be like if Liam looked at her with so much affection? What would it be like if he ever chose to devote that same close attention to her as a woman, not just as a woman he still saw as the little girl who'd grown up while he was on tour? She wanted that more than anything, wished she had someone to lean on like that, wished Liam would be that person.

Sighing, she reminded herself for what seemed like the hundredth time that he didn't see her as a potential girlfriend or spouse. She was just the friend who gave him a chance to do something charitable here and there. He helped out of duty, not romantic affection, and as easy as it was to forget that in moments like these, she couldn't afford to forget that. Not when it would crush her heart to come back to reality if she let her dreams take her too far.

If only he had been Trystam's father, then she'd have him by her side, and she could be certain he didn't look at her as a little girl he felt responsible for.

Chapter 4

Liam received a call from the front desk informing him that Mr. Marlin had stopped in and requested to see him. He pinched the bridge of his nose with a sigh. His men gave him regular updates now that they'd often contracted out the detective work to a firm he'd worked with and moved Marlin to the safe house. He knew everything happening, particularly that Marlin was a nightmare to deal with—little surprise there. The man was petulant, spoiled, and on a power trip. He needed to be knocked down a peg, but he was a client, so with nothing more than his own pride at stake, Liam had kept his mouth shut.

The last thing he wanted was to see the pushy, obnoxious DA, but appointment or not, the man had pull and was a high-paying client. He didn't have any meetings right now and could spare thirty minutes or so. "Send him up," he told the front desk with a sigh. "Maddie will let him into my office."

He hoped the man wouldn't bully his assistant in any way. The staff on the first floor had complained about him last time he'd dropped in for the initial meeting, and he didn't want Maddie harassed.

To be certain she didn't have any trouble, he waited until he heard the elevator ding and closed out his work to go greet Marlin himself.

He reached the outer office to see Marlin standing stock still at the threshold of the office space, staring at Maddie. For her part, Maddie looked like she'd seen a ghost. She pushed away from the desk with trembling legs and forced herself to stand. "I...are you in the appointment books, sir?"

Liam was impressed at her ability to rally from what was so obviously a shock––though he didn't know why she was behaving that way––but he didn't want this going any further. He cleared his throat.

Maddie jumped and whirled about, eyes wide. If he'd thought she was pale before, she was practically white now. Her hands shook at her sides, and she looked between Marlin and him like a deer caught in the headlights. "I...I didn't hear you come out, sir."

"I can see that." Liam narrowed his eyes, examining Marlin's change in posture.

The man didn't look nearly as pushy as usual. He hadn't demanded his meeting either. In fact, he was still standing in frozen silence as if he didn't quite know what to do. When he noticed Liam's glance, he snapped out of it and returned to his usual blustery, obnoxious self. "Yes, I am in the appointment book, woman. Obviously, I am, or they wouldn't have sent me up."

Maddie flinched, her gaze falling to the floor. "Of c-course. I'm s-sorry. I didn't catch your name. Maybe there was some mistake. I j-just didn't see the appointment, that's all. I'm sure...It's probably...I didn't..."

Marlin glared at her. "Can you manage a single sentence without stuttering? Do you have any idea how annoying it is?"

She flushed, tears sparkling in her gaze as she lifted her gaze to Liam's in a wordless plea.

"Can't you hire decent help, Mr. Beckett. She certainly doesn't inspire confidence." Marlin tucked his hands into his pockets, a vicious smile on his lips. "She never has."

His eyes narrowed. This man knew her somehow. Maddie hurried to the computer, fingers shaking too violently to unlock it. When that failed, she turned to the paper record of the appointment book she kept, but she couldn't seem to locate whatever she was looking for.

Liam's fists clenched. How dare Marlin come in here and mistreat his staff, barge in uninvited and unannounced, and then criticize his secretary as if she'd been the one in the wrong? That it was Maddie, who struggled with harsh criticism and her own self-doubts, only increased his fury. "Mr. Marlin," he snapped. "Get out."

Marlin stared in shocked silence for a moment. "Excuse me?" he finally managed.

"Get. Out."

"You're kicking a paying client out over your secretary? Over *her?*" Marlin glowered at him.

Liam wasn't budging on this one. "You insulted my staff, and now you're insulting my ability to choose my staff wisely. Miss Hayes is a valued member of our staff."

Maddie quivered as she fought to keep herself under control. Liam walked over and wrapped his arm around her waist, pulling her into his side and hiding her face. His anger burned higher.

"I came for an update, and I'm paying your paycheck! You'll not kick me out over a snotty, over-sensitive woman."

"I'll kick you out because of your behavior towards my secretary and have now royally ticked me off!" Liam roared in response. "Get out before I tear up our contract and have security drag you off the premises and kick you to the curb."

Maddie shivered in his arms. He pet her hair gently and rubbed her back, trying to convey silently that he wasn't angry with her, but over the poor treatment she'd received.

Marlin shot him a nasty glare, but he spun around and marched back into the elevator. "This isn't over, Maddie. We have a lot of catching up to do, apparently. Where is the snot-nosed brat you insisted you'd keep? Or did you change your mind after all?"

When Maddie went still and tense, Liam finally put it together. He swore and released Maddie. "Marlin, if you're not gone in the next five seconds and out of my office building soon after, you're losing my protection. I don't care how much you pay me. You just made this personal, and if you want me to remain professional, you'll do what I say. Now."

The man huffed and punched the elevator button. The doors closed off their view of his annoyed expression, leaving him alone with Maddie, who was now slumped in her chair with her hands buried in her face. "I'm s-sorry." Her breath hitched. "I'm s-sorry, Liam."

He crouched in front of her and pulled her hands away from her face. "There's nothing to be sorry for, missy. He's gone. You're okay. You're okay." He reached out and wiped away her tears with his thumbs. "Deep breaths, Maddie."

She relaxed into his soothing touch with a shiver. He opened his arms for her, and she fell into his embrace without hesitation, curling into him and burying her face in his chest.

"He's Trystam's father, isn't he?" Liam asked.

The tension returned, and she tried to wiggle out of his grip. He pinched her hip in warning and tightened his grasp. "Oh, no, you don't, missy. You've avoided this with me for far too long already, and look where it's put us. I'm stuck with a client I have even more reason to hate now that I know what he's done, and I can't drop him without good reason. This doesn't count. You've been reduced to a quivering mess. Was he always this mean when you two were together?"

She shook her head, settling in his lap with a resigned sigh. "He had moments, but he never spoke to me quite like that. He...sometimes scolded me or yelled at me for embarrassing him in front of friends by talking too much or getting nervous and stammering. He could be really mean if he'd been drinking, but he...he wasn't like this sober."

Liam rubbed soothing circles into her hip with his thumb, fighting the urge to go after the other man to give him a lesson in how to treat women. "I'm glad he's not with you and Trystam, then."

"He's changed, Liam," she whispered. "He scares me. What if he insists on seeing Trystam now that he knows where we are?"

"I don't think there's any reason to worry about that, sweetheart," he murmured. "He didn't want anything to do with you and Trystam before. Why start now?"

"I don't want to see him again."

"Don't worry. I won't be letting him near you in this office." Liam kissed the top of her head. "Come on. We're going out for lunch and a coffee. I think we still have quite a while until my next meeting, and you need time to recuperate."

She let him lead her to the elevator without protest and didn't even object to the way he kept her cuddled close to his side the whole way down, which told him just how scared of Marlin she was. He gritted his teeth and swore he'd do whatever he had to in order to keep Marlin away from her.

***

Later that evening, Maddie put Trystam down to bed and poured herself a glass of wine to steady her still frayed nerves after the encounter with Alyx Marlin. She'd never imagined he would resurface or that he would show up at her place of work, of all places. In fact, she'd come to hope never to see him again at all. She had sole custody of Trystam, but seeing him again dredged up old worries about a custody battle if he ever walked back into their lives. Now he was apparently a DA a few counties over and held a lot of sway. He was also meaner, and Maddie didn't for a second think he wouldn't be more inclined to make people's lives hell if he didn't like something they'd done.

She sipped at the wine and settled onto the couch to turn on the TV. Just as she switched it on, there was a knock at the door. She frowned and checked her cell. Liam usually texted if he was coming over, and he rarely visited after Trystam was in bed, though he'd been doing a lot of things he rarely did over the last few days. He'd touched her more in the last week or two than he had in years of friendship since his return from Iraq six years ago.

There was no text, but she got up at the second insistent knock and trudged over to open the door. "It's an odd hour to visit."

"Really? It's barely after seven," a familiar, nasally voice snapped.

She gasped and tried to slam the door on him. Alyx reached out and grabbed it, leveraging it open with surprising strength. Not wanting a scene to wake Trystam or to deal with cops on her doorstep tonight, she gave in and let him in. "What do you want?" she snapped.

"I came to find out where the kid is. You might want to keep me out, Madison, but Trystam is my son too. I want to be part of his life."

"And where were you the past five years?" she snapped. "He has a father, and it isn't you."

"Is it Liam Hayes?" Alyx snorted. "Really, Madison. With your boss? I knew you'd sink low, but not that low."

She lifted her chin, tears threatening. "Get out, Alyx. I'm not sleeping with Liam. He's a good man and a good friend. He did what you should have for me and Trystam."

Alyx rolled his eyes. "Really? You think I owed you anything? I told you I wasn't ready for a kid, and I told you I had this great ADA position lined up. I was too close to have that derailed by a kid. You were pretty close to finishing up your own degree in accounting too, but I guess you gave it up for a snot-nosed brat. Now look where you are."

His gaze wandered around the small house she'd rented in derision, and she looked at it in shame for the first time. She'd never once felt so embarrassed by the small place she'd managed to rent to give Trystam a safe neighborhood to grow up in, not even when Liam or Jessica visited. They probably had twice the amount of money Alyx had, but he made her feel small in ways they never had.

"The kid could use a parent who can provide for him. I can do that now." He modulated his tone. "Be reasonable, Madison. He deserves to know his father, and a little child support wouldn't hurt anything, would it?"

Maddie flinched. "We're doing fine on our own," she whispered.

"Fine. You're doing fine," he scoffed, spreading his hands in a placating gesture. "But shouldn't Trystam get to meet his father? I'm sure he has questions."

He did. A lot of them now that he was getting old enough to understand that his situation was different from that of the children he went to school with. When the teacher talked about mommies and daddies and asked the children to share about their parents, Trystam either refused to participate or told them about Liam before bursting into tears. She'd had to leave work early to collect him a few times because of the issue.

A gleam entered Alyx's eye. "He does, doesn't he?"

She hunched her shoulders and wrapped her arms around her midsection. "Alyx, I..."

He reached out and took her chin in his slender fingers. "Stand up straight and look me in the eye. You know I hate it when people slouch and avoid looking me in the eye. Have a modicum of self-respect, Madison."

She flinched away from his touch. "D-don't touch me."

He smirked. "Stuttering again? You've forgotten everything I taught you when we were together and all the rules, too, apparently. But that's all right, *Maddie*. You'll relearn them. Go wake the kid up. I know he's here. You've glanced at the stairs every few seconds since I arrived."

Had she? She cringed, hating that she'd given away his presence to a man she didn't trust. "Please just let him sleep, Alyx," she whispered. "Come by another day at an hour when he's awake. Then you can meet him."

He nodded. "Tomorrow. Six sharp. I'll bring dinner."

She bit her lip and stared at the floor, unable to bring herself to answer or meet his eyes. Apparently an answer wasn't needed. He strode out of the house without bothering to confirm the time worked, leaving her alone in the living room.

She sank onto the sofa and knocked back the rest of her wine, tears burning her eyes and then slipping over her cheeks. She wanted to call Liam, but this wasn't the sort of thing she could tell him over the phone, so she resisted the urge and curled up to cry out the stress and anxiety of having Alyx here left inside.

Chapter 5

Liam knew something was wrong the moment Maddie walked into the office. She had dark bags under her eyes and looked like she'd been crying. He pushed away from his desk and strode out to hers. She handed him his coffee wordlessly, keeping her face carefully turned away from him.

He took the coffee and set it down on the desk. "What's wrong, Maddie?"

She tensed.

"Madison Hayes," he snapped. "We've known each other long enough to be honest with one another. Saying nothing isn't any better than lying to me in my books. If you don't want to tell me, then you tell me that. To my face."

She twisted her hands on the edges of her sweater. "Alyx visited last night."

Silence dropped over the two of them. He shoved away from the desk and raked his fingers through his hair. "I...what did he want?" He forced the words out, forcing his jaw to loosen enough to let the question escape as he paced away from the desk.

"He wanted back into Trystam's life. Insisted, in fact."

"Did he hurt you?" Liam hissed, stalking back to her.

She wouldn't meet his gaze. "Not really. He just scared me, and I was...I made him go away."

"How did you make him go away?" Liam's eyes narrowed.

"I told him he could see Trystam another day."

"There's more than that, isn't there, missy?" He crossed his arms. "Out with it."

"He wants to bring dinner over tomorrow."

Liam lost his temper at that. "Like hell he will."

Maddie's eyes widened at his cursing, something he restrained from doing around her. "He didn't wait for me to agree or refuse. He just sort of assumed I would..."

"Then he's going to have one more *unexpected* guest. I'm not leaving you two alone with him."

Maddie's gaze dropped to the gray carpet. "Why does it matter to you so much, Liam? He hasn't hurt us. I...I don't think he will as long as he gets a part in Trystam's life."

"And you think a man like that is safe for your son?" He knelt in front of her and covered her tiny hands with his. "Maddie, I love that kid like my own."

She looked away, disappointment flashing across her expression, but she didn't respond. Did she want to hear him say he loved her? Well, it was a good time for a confession anyway. He wasn't letting her give in to Alyx without making it clear she could choose him, choose a man who would cherish and care for her instead of frightening and threatening her.

"Look at me, Maddie," he ordered.

Her gaze snapped back to his.

"I love you too."

"Like a friend, I know," she mumbled. "I know you're just worried about what he might do, but really, I don't—"

He leaned up and stopped the flow of words with his mouth. He'd never been good with words, preferring actions to make his point. He'd learned to express himself verbally, too, of course, but right now, he didn't think verbal would cut it. She wouldn't listen, or she'd find reasons he didn't mean what he'd said.

She whimpered and relaxed into his touch with a soft sigh. When he tangled his fingers in her hair, she groaned and let him deepen the kiss without any protest. She'd definitely wanted this for a while. He'd suspected as much, but Maddie had been reluctant to show her emotions or her desires ever since Alyx deserted her with a baby on the way. He'd come home to a much shyer, nerdier, quieter version of her, though he'd quickly discovered how easily she babbled when nervous. He didn't dislike that version of Madison Hayes—far from it—but he missed the little girl whose emotions could be read on her face like words on a page. He hated that she felt any need to hide, at least with him.

There was no hiding now, though. She pressed against him, hands sliding up to his shoulders to anchor her against him. He had no intention of letting her go any time soon, but he didn't want to get too carried away. The first time he let that happen would be in his bed, not up against her desk where anyone could see if they walked by. He released her with a regretful sigh.

She lifted her fingers to touch her lips, eyes wide.

"Not like a friend," he murmured.

"Not like a friend."

Her agreement brought a smile to his face. "Glad I finally got that across, missy. Took long enough. Maybe now you can understand why I hate the idea of you being anywhere with Alyx alone. Besides, the man is petty, mean, and drunk on his own power. You shouldn't be left with him alone."

"But...you c-can't just show up to dinner without an invitation," she protested.

"Little girl, I most certainly can, and that is precisely what I'll do. I don't care if it's rude. This is about your safety and well-being. Can you honestly tell me you want him in your home near your son and you with no one else around?"

She lowered her gaze to the floor and lifted one shoulder half-heartedly.

"Words," he murmured.

"No. I can't."

"I didn't think so." He reached out and tipped her chin up.

"Maddie, please. Let me show you that I'm worth the chance."

She chewed on her lower lip. "I...I want to, but he's Trystam's father."

Liam scowled and crossed his arms. "And? He's nothing but the biological father, the one who donated his half and then left you with the responsibility for the result. He hasn't been here for you or for Trystam. He didn't care what had happened to you or the baby, and he taunted you with it yesterday as I kicked him out of the office. He doesn't want a second chance. He sees an opportunity to wheedle his way back into your lives for whatever selfish reason. Maybe he does want to know Trystam. Maybe Trystam is just an excuse to get you back. A man like that must hate knowing he lost something so precious."

"I...He..."

Liam raised a brow.

"Okay, he was like that when we were dating, too," she mumbled, gaze returning to the floor. "But...I can't tell him no to seeing his son, Liam. He...He does have a right."

"Says who? You have sole custody."

"But not officially. Legally, Alyx can still fight me on this. He's the sort who would fight me over it if I dug my heels in and gave him a reason. This way, maybe he'll get bored and leave when he sees I won't put out."

Liam sighed and tipped his head toward his office. "Come on. We'll continue this in my office where no one will disturb us."

She followed him inside and shut the door. "You won't take no for an answer on dinner, will you?"

"I will not," he confirmed. "But whether we go anywhere is entirely up to you. You know now that I do want you that way, and if I'm not mistaken, you *really* want to."

She wouldn't meet his gaze and rolled her lips together like she often did when she was nervous and unsure.

"Hey. Look at me, Maddie."

She did, though reluctantly.

"I'm still the same guy you've known all these years. Why are you nervous?"

"I don't know what to do." Tears filled her eyes. "I...I want to say yes, but I'm afraid if I do, he'll...he'll be angry."

"Let me handle him. Tell me what you want, not what you think you have to do to avoid his anger."

"I want you," she whispered.

"You can have me."

"But I don't feel like I can."

"Then give me a chance to change those feelings." He stepped forward and cupped her cheek in his hand. "It's simple, Maddie. Let me lead. All you have to do is take a tiny step of faith to have what you want. I promise."

She searched his gaze for a long moment, lower lip caught between her teeth. Then she nodded. "Okay."

He bent his head and kissed her once more, this time more chastely. "Thank you. I'll be at dinner."

Chapter 6

Liam showed up a half-hour before Alyx was scheduled to arrive. She let him in with a sigh, relaxing into his solid embrace after he closed the door. Trystam looked up from where he was coloring on the floor and grinned. "Mommy, is Liam staying for dinner?"

Liam smiled back at the little boy. "Yes, I am. But Trystam, I need to talk to you about something. Do you think you could listen closely for me?"

She shot him a worried look, but he shook his head slightly, a silent command not to intervene, to trust him with this. Well, trusting him had never gone wrong before. She settled back into his side and turned her attention back to her son.

The little boy's smile had dropped, replaced with a serious look, and he nodded. "'Course I can."

Liam released her and took her hand, pulling her over to the couch. He settled her down and then sat on the floor with Trystam. "Trystam, there are two things you need to know. One, I love you and your mommy very much. But you already know that, don't you?"

The five-year-old shrugged. "Yeah. Mommy doesn't like it when I tell everyone at school you're my daddy, but you don't mind, do you?"

Liam laughed. "No, I don't. In fact, I'm honored that you've chosen to give me that position. But you know, I love your mommy as more than just a friend."

"Like...Love, love, right?" Trystam frowned. "Like giving her a valentine?"

"Yes, like that." He glanced over at Maddie.

She felt the heat rising in her cheeks. Was he seriously trying to explain that they were dating to her son?

"Your mommy is one stubborn woman, and it's taken a lot of convincing, but she's agreed to give me a chance to be more than just a friend. Do you understand what that means?"

Trystam's frown deepened. "Like you want to be my daddy for real?"

"Eventually, but your mother hasn't agreed to that yet."

Maddie made a tiny sound of protest, but she didn't intervene when he looked over and raised a brow. He still wanted her to trust him, and Trystam didn't seem upset or worried by the prospect, though he did seem a little unsure of how to process it. Liam wasn't going to share anything the child shouldn't know. She burrowed deeper into the couch as her son also looked at her, his expression inquisitive. This wasn't how she'd envisioned this conversation happening at all.

"Maddie?" he murmured. "I'm not going to hide our relationship from your son. Nor will I hide my intentions. He deserves to know."

She bit her lower lip, but she nodded in agreement. Liam was right. They couldn't be sneaking around or pretending nothing had changed. If things worked and became serious—and deep down, she really hoped they would—then Trystam would need to know eventually. Better to give him time to adjust gradually.

"Trystam, someday, I do want to marry your mom and become your real daddy. But for now, I'm settling for being something between that and just a friend. She needs time to decide what she wants too."

Trystam nodded solemnly. "What's the second thing?"

"The second thing is that your biological father wants to meet you. He'll be here soon for dinner."

Trystam scowled. "I heard him talking to Mommy at the door last night. I don't like him."

Maddie sucked in a sharp breath. "Trystam! How many times have I told you not to eavesdrop?"

"Sorry, Mommy." The child gave her a contrite look. "But I heard the bell, and I thought maybe it was Liam."

"So what? I put you to bed." Maddie crossed her arms. "I expected you to go to sleep and stay put."

"I couldn't sleep. Tomorrow is field trip day to the zoo, and I was thinking about all the animals we'd see." Trystam pouted. "I couldn't go to sleep, and then the doorbell rang."

She sighed. "I'm not mad, Trystam. But your biological father is..."

"Mean," Trystam muttered.

"Hey! Do we name call in this house?"

"No." Her son cast her a mutinous glare. "But he deserves it."

"I'm with Trystam on this one," Liam murmured. "I think it's a fair assessment."

She huffed. "Fine...he's mean. That just means it's important you're careful around him, Trystam. You can't tell him about Liam and me. If he asks, tell him Liam's just a friend, and you can't tell him you tell anyone at school Liam's your daddy, understood?"

"Will he hurt us if I mess up, Mommy?"

She slid down to the floor and gathered her son up in her arms, tears threatening. Clutching him close, she stared at Liam over her child's head. He smiled reassuringly.

"No, baby," she murmured, kissing the top of his head. "He's not going to hurt us. Liam won't let him, and neither will I. That's why he's here. To protect us if something goes wrong."

The little boy wrapped his arms around her waist and held her tightly. "Okay."

The doorbell rang, putting an end to the conversation.

"Is that him?" Trystam murmured.

"Probably." Liam glanced at his watch. "He said six sharp, didn't he?"

Maddie nodded, moving to get up.

"Stay there." Liam stood and headed for the door. "Might as well let him know right now that there's one more person coming to dinner." He yanked the door open.

Alyx stood on the doorstep, grocery bags in hand. When he saw Liam, his expression morphed from ingratiating to furious in a split second. "What the hell are you doing here?"

Liam crossed his arms. "I came over to check on Maddie. You upset her yesterday."

Alyx glowered past Liam at her. "Did you tell him I visited, Madison?"

She held Trystam a little closer, flinching even though she knew Liam wouldn't let him do anything.

"You did." He shook his head. "You little..."

"I suggest you don't finish that sentence if you want to come in for dinner as planned."

Alyx turned his fury on Liam. "I didn't bring enough for a fourth person," he snapped.

"That's fine. I can figure something out."

"Madison, tell him to leave."

Maddie shivered at the cold tone in Alyx's voice, and Trystam trembled against her. "He's a friend, Alyx. I...I forgot about dinner when I told him he could come over."

"Then it shouldn't be a problem for him to leave if he's been visiting for a while."

"I'm not going anywhere. I said I'd figure out my own food. I did *not* say I'd be leaving." Liam stepped aside. "Do you want help with the groceries?"

"No." Alyx sneered at him. "I don't need my bodyguard helping with anything. Not the food, and certainly not my family."

Liam's expression remained cold and stony. He didn't contradict Alyx, but he also didn't acquiesce. He merely shut the door while Alyx stalked into the kitchen and then walked over to take Trystam from Maddie. The little boy wrapped his arms around Liam's neck and buried his face in Liam's broad shoulder. Maddie wished she could hide from this mess just as easily, but that wasn't an option.

"I'll go help in the kitchen."

"We all will. Trystam," he murmured to the little boy. "Remember what we said? Can you be a big boy for us and play nice with your father?"

Trystam huffed in annoyance. "I don't wanna."

"I know. None of us do, but we need you to be all grown up tonight. Please?"

"You really want me to play nice?" Trystam asked.

"I do. Tell you what. Play nice, and I'll take you to the water park with your mom this Saturday."

"Deal."

Liam let the boy down and gave him a gentle nudge toward the kitchen. Trystam wandered in and started a conversation with Alyx. To his credit, Alyx responded politely without the acidity in his tone he'd had when talking to Liam and Maddie. She and Liam joined the two in the kitchen, and a tense silence spread over the small space. Maddie closed her eyes. Well, this was going to be one long evening.

Chapter 7

Liam met Maddie at her doorstep. His hands were tucked into his pockets. She'd worn a modest one piece with a pair of shorts, but he couldn't help letting his imagination wander. When they were done with the water park today, he'd be certain to convince her to stay over at his place with Trystam. He wanted her in his bed under his roof, especially knowing that Alyx had kept stopping by when he wasn't around and that the visits had left Maddie more stressed out.

She looked more relaxed today than he'd seen her all week. Trystam bounced out the door, pausing only briefly to wrap his arms around Liam's legs in greeting before racing for the car, his towel tightly wrapped around his waist, goggles in hand. Maddie shook her head, and Liam laughed. "Hasn't he ever been to a water park?"

She shook her head. "No."

"No wonder he's so excited." He leaned in and kissed her gently, enjoying the way she relaxed into him. "Come stay at my place tonight."

"But Alyx—"

"Screw Alyx," he murmured. "You need a break, and I promised you that if you'd let me, I'd show you what it was like to be with a man who actually respected and cared for you. This is part of that."

She chewed on the inside of her cheek. "What if he's—"

"Angry?" Liam raised a brow.

She blushed a pretty pink.

"You really have to stop saying that. It's not a very good excuse."

"It isn't an excuse," she protested. "I'm worried he's going to sue for joint custody, and I don't want Trystam anywhere near him."

"Come on, Mommy!" Trystam hollered.

Liam turned to level the boy with a stern glare. "Trystam Hayes, the water park will still be there in a few more minutes. Do not yell across the driveway or interrupt adults when they're speaking unless there is a legitimate emergency."

The boy squirmed in the car, but he eventually nodded. "Sorry, Liam," he called back more softly.

"Apology accepted." He sighed and turned back to Maddie with a shake of his head. "Come on, missy. Say yes. I can handle Alyx. You've been dealing with him all week, and don't say it hasn't been stressful or exhausting. I can see it in your face at work."

"I guess I'm losing my touch if you can read me so easily," she joked weakly.

"We all reach a point where we can't hide our emotions anymore. I hate seeing you hit a point where you're so stressed and worn down that you can't even put on a convincing front with others who don't know you well. Even the receptionist who helps out when you're out for the day has asked if you should be told to take a vacation day."

She flushed. "Is it that obvious?"

"Yes, it is. Say yes, Maddie. You'll feel better with a place that's away from him and his pestering for a weekend."

She smiled shyly. "We won't be intruding, will we? I know the weekends are your only real downtime."

"I would be delighted to have you there. It's a little too quiet around my place sometimes. Since Jessica moved down to Miami for work, she hasn't visited as much, and it gets lonely."

"Okay. We'll stay. Should I pack a bag?"

"I think we've made Trystam wait long enough." Liam glanced at the little boy, who was waiting patiently, if not all that quietly.

Trystam bounced up and down in his seat and pulled his goggles on. He didn't sit still once, even when he realized Liam was looking at him with a wry smile.

"He's about to burst with excitement. Jessica won't mind if you use the things she's left lying around in the guest room, and Trystam has some things there from the last time you were over to stay with me and Jessica."

"All right." Her shoulders slumped, the tension he'd seen all week vanishing in a wave of grateful relief. Some of the usual spark of life returned to her face, and she offered him a genuine smile. "Thank you, Liam. You...You always look out for us. I really do appreciate it. More than you know."

He reached out and tugged on her braid affectionately. "And I will continue doing so for as long as you let me, missy. Ready for the water park?"

She nodded eagerly, her own mood escalating from relief to actual enthusiasm. "You know, I've never been to one either. My parents never had the money."

"Then it'll be a treat for you too." He took her hand and drew her toward the car, taking the swim bag from her shoulder and carrying it for her.

She held onto his hand tightly the whole way to the car. He pulled away to put the swim bag in the trunk and then climbed into the driver's seat.

Once they were on the road, he held her hand the whole way to the water park while Trystam colored in the back and sang along to the kids' songs Maddie played on her phone for him.

This was the perfect moment.

All of them together, all of them happy and not thinking about any of the worries from the week. He'd do anything to have these sorts of moments with Maddie for the rest of his life.

***

The park was a hit with Trystam and Maddie. The three of them flopped onto a bench to indulge in a funnel cake after a morning of slides and fun in the water. Trystam ate his third of the cake enthusiastically, watching all park visitors as they passed by, kids tugging at adults' hands as they hurried for the next ride.

He seemed content to sit and watch under the umbrella over the table, but he also seemed tired and sleepy.

Liam settled Maddie on his lap, ignoring the blush creeping up her neck as she glanced nervously at the people passing by. No one paid any attention, focused entirely on their own day.

He pressed a kiss to her shoulder and reached for the funnel cake, offering her a bite.

Her cheeks heated further, but she took the offered food with a shy smile. "Thank you. This is nice, Liam."

"Someone needs to spoil you. It's not like you do it yourself."

"Well, I...it's not like I have time."

"Precisely. Which just means I get to spoil you that much more. I'm not going to complain about that." He fed her another bite of the funnel cake.

Trystam rested his head on his arms, still watching the people even as his eyelids drooped.

"I think someone's ready for a nap."

"No, I'm fine!" Trystam protested. "We don't have to go."

"We can always come back another day, little man," Liam murmured. "But I think both you and your mother are tired."

As if to underscore the point, Trystam yawned, and Maddie let her back rest more heavily against Liam's chest.

"You're going to fall asleep right here at the table, kiddo," Maddie agreed. "Another day. We'll find time to go on the rest of the slides, okay?"

"Okay," he mumbled reluctantly. "You promise?"

"Promise," Liam told him.

Trystam yawned again. "Then I guess I could go home."

"We're going back to my place, actually." Liam lifted Maddie off his lap and stood. "Your mom needs a break, so I told her you two could come over. Is that okay?"

The little boy perked up a bit, looking a tiny bit less tired. "Really? Can I play with the Xbox again?"

"Of course you can." Liam laughed. "It doesn't see much use from me these days. Someone should play with it. But you're taking a nap first, and so are your mother and I. Everyone needs a little rest after this morning."

Trystam nodded agreeably. He took Liam's offered hand and walked alongside him to the exit of the park.

Liam bundled the child into the back seat of his car in the parking lot, buckling him in.

Maddie put the swim bag in the back and headed for her door. He opened it and helped her in, too, buckling her seatbelt before she could protest and dropping a kiss on her forehead. She smiled up at him with a sleepy, contented expression in her eyes. By the time he got back to his place, both mother and son were asleep.

Chapter 8

Maddie opened her eyes and stretched with a yawn. Liam looked up from his book and smiled at her. He remained settled comfortably against the pillows on his side of the bed, where he'd been when she'd fallen asleep this afternoon. Jessica had taken Trystam out for the afternoon to give them time alone, but she'd been so exhausted from work and dealing with Alyx that she'd had no energy for anything but a nap. A glance at the clock confirmed they only had a few hours before Trystam would be bouncing through the door, excited about wherever "Auntie Jess", as he called Maddie's best friend, had taken him.

Liam closed the book gently and set it aside. He took her chin in his hand and kissed her softly. "Welcome back to the land of the living, Sleeping Beauty."

She laughed and leaned up for a fuller kiss. "I'm sorry I fell asleep on you. What were you reading?"

"A spy novel. I needed a break from looking at reports and emails from your would-be suitor."

She scowled at the mention of Alyx. "At least he only bothers you with emails."

Liam frowned. "Is he bothering you? I know he stresses you out, but I thought things had been better the last few weeks. I've had the guys keep a tighter leash on him with the whole stalker and gang-related threats."

Shrugging, she burrowed into his side and rested her head on his shoulder. "He still comes over to see us. He's rude when Trystam's not around and seems interested in nothing but his son or ridiculing me for how I'm parenting."

Liam's frown deepened as he met her gaze. "I don't like that you let him come to your house."

"He's Trystam's father. I—"

"Have to," he grumbled. "So you've said. But you wouldn't have to if you moved on. Moved *in* with me," he murmured. "He's not going to push it with me. I have more connections than he does, thanks to how long I've been at this game."

"Move in?" She hummed sleepily. "I like the sound of it, but we're...we're still trying to figure out what we are to each other."

He slid a hand around her hip, sliding it just under her t-shirt. "*We* are not still trying to figure that out. You are. I know what I want."

"I..." She shifted under the warm, calloused touch of his fingers. "I don't know for sure what it is you want."

"No?" A wicked gleam entered his gaze, and he smirked. "Seems I haven't done a very good job of communicating then, baby girl. I want you. Plain and simple. However I can have you. I've been giving you space and haven't pushed you toward anything we haven't already discussed, but don't mistake that for reluctance on my part. There will never be a time when I don't want you, Maddie Hayes."

Her cheeks warmed, and she tried to bury her face in his chest with a shy laugh. "I never would've taken you for a sweet talker, Liam."

"I'm not." He removed his hand only to grip her by the waist and lift her to straddle his lap. "I am a man of action. If you really want to know what I want, what I'm looking for, I'm all for showing you."

She chewed on her lower lip, pressing her palms to his chest. "I don't know...Trystam—"

"Isn't here." He leaned in and nipped her earlobe. "Because my sister wanted to give us a little time alone. Probably figured we'd get to this sooner or later. She would never guess how shy you are about this stuff, little girl."

"You're not going to tell her, either!" She squirmed in spite of her sharp tone, unable to deny that what he was doing felt wonderful and, more importantly, right, like he fit her in a way Alyx never had and never would.

"No," he agreed. "I'm not."

She settled a little at that promise, sighing. "Do you really want me? Baggage and all?"

"I don't see baggage. I see beauty." He trailed his lips along the column of her throat. "And I see strength. You never see any of that, but I want to show you I do today. You promised you'd let me show you what it was like to let a real man love you."

"I've...I've kept that promise."

"I have one more thing I want to show you before I ask you for a commitment, Madison," he whispered against her collarbones. "Let me love you this way too. Let me wash away what he did and show you what it should be like. I...I need to erase him, destroy the lingering hurt over what he did to you. I need to show you your scars are a reminder of your strengths, not his cruelty."

She groaned and leaned closer, wrapping her arms around his neck. "How can I say no when you say that sort of stuff, Liam?"

He lifted his head, gaze vulnerable in a way she hadn't seen before. "Do you want to say no?"

She shook her head and lowered her mouth to his. Nothing in her wanted to say no. Everything in her wanted this man and all that he was. For this brief moment, she didn't need to worry about Alyx. Liam could be her whole world, if only for a moment. If only he could be her world forever, though. If only Alyx would disappear so that she would be free to love without repercussions. But he couldn't, and Alyx wouldn't, so she—like Liam—would take what she could get and hold onto it with a fierce protectiveness to cherish it forever.

***

When she returned home that night with Trystam, the cloud of euphoria and contentment she'd been floating on since being with Liam evaporated in a moment. Alyx sat on the doorstep, looking furious. He modulated the expression to one of subtle anger when he spotted Trystam with her, forcing a smile for the child's sake and sending the boy inside with a promise he wouldn't hold up Maddie for long.

Maddie crossed her arms and scowled. "What are you doing here?"

"Don't you ever check your phone?" he snapped. "You're as bad as you were when we were dating. Worse, actually, because now you're screwing around with some other guy." He looked her over contemptuously. "Wasn't I enough for you?"

"You *left* me, Alyx. Left me with a baby on the way so you could go to law school. And don't expect me to believe you didn't lay a few girls over the years, either. At least when I finally decided to sleep with him, I did so after being certain I was more than a one-night stand. Did the girls you slept with even care?"

His cheeks mottled red. "You've slept with him?" His voice lowered to a hissing whisper, and he took a menacing step forward. "It's bad enough that my son looks at him like a father, but now *you* slept with him?"

She balled her hands into fists and forced herself not to take a step backward. Every time they'd argued before, she'd caved. Alyx had his way every time, and she'd always made excuses. She wasn't making them for him anymore. If he couldn't take her boundaries or the fact that she had no intention of being with him again, he could leave. "You don't get to dictate who I'm with," she snapped back. "At least he's been the only one. How many have you had over the years?"

"As many as I pleased." He sneered at her. "Unlike you, I don't view being a prude as a worthy ideal."

She refused to take the bait and crossed her arms. "Go home, Alyx. I don't want you here."

"Too bad. I came to tell you I'm going to file a motion for partial custody of Trystam. He should have his father in his life."

"You are in his life."

"For now. When I go back to my usual position, I'll be two hours from here. I don't have time to be coming up for visits all the time. I'm guessing you won't bring him to me on your own, so I want weekends."

"No."

"That's precisely why I plan to file a motion. It'll be filed in a few weeks when I have the room to go public with it."

She lost it then, anger and fear driving her. "How dare you? I've been raising my son for five years without you! You can't even bother to come down on the weekends to visit him, so you want to take him away from me to make your life easier! What sort of father does that? You're a narcissistic piece of work, Alyx, and I have no intention of giving you my son any more than I intend to come back to you!"

He grabbed her wrist and dragged her closer, pulling her inside. "Lower your voice if you don't want your son to hear."

She ground her teeth, muscles trembling with the struggle not to deck him.

He pushed her up against the wall, hand going to her hip. "You won't be seeing Mr. Beckett again. Not when you have my son under your roof. I am the only man he will see you with, the only man he will ever call 'daddy' again. I know he tells the kids at school that Beckett is his father. That's going to end. You'll make it end." His grip on her wrist squeezed until she had to bite her lip to hold back a pained whimper. "If you don't obey me on this, I am going to take full custody of Trystam. You'll never see him again. You know what I do for a living, Madison. You know I could do it with a simple word to the judge."

Tears of pain and rage welled up. "You stay away from my son," she hissed.

"Oh, Madison." He reached up and wiped the tears away with a bitter smile. "You brought this on yourself, my dear. You should have known better than to keep the boy, and you should have known I wouldn't want my only living heir to grow up in this sort of tasteless place. If you'd done a better job raising him, I might not have been pushed to this. And if you weren't sleeping around with your *boss*, maybe I'd trust you to behave without this threat hanging over your head. But you are living in this little hole in the ground neighborhood, and you are frequenting Beckett's bed, so you see why I have to intervene."

"What I see is that you're a selfish pig!"

He released her wrist, and she thought he was going to move away. Instead, his hand snapped across her cheek, setting a fire blazing there. She was too stunned to cry. Instead, she dropped to her knees, her hand going to her injured cheek while she cradled the sprained, aching wrist he'd held to her chest. He sneered down at her, hands on his hips. "I think I've made myself clear, Madison. Clean yourself up and go change the sheets on your bed. I'm sure they smell like him, and I don't plan on sleeping on sheets he's used."

Terror closed around her chest like a vice, squeezing the air from her lungs. The tears flowed in earnest, and she huddled there without moving. He sighed and bent over, grabbing her by the injured wrist and forcing her to her feet. She cried out softly at the pain but tried to stay quiet so that Trystam wouldn't come to investigate. When she looked to the stairs of the small house, though, she saw him watching. She looked away, trying not to draw Alyx's attention to the boy.

"Alyx, be reasonable," she whispered. "You're under protective custody to keep the thugs after you from finding you. Think about the danger you'll be in if you stay in an unsecured location, the danger you'd be putting Trystam in. Please..."

He released with a disgusted huff. "Fine. It seems more thinking goes on in that head of yours than it used to. I'll arrange things and return in the morning. Don't even think of running, or I'll have the cops on you for child abduction."

She trembled and backed away. "I...I'm not going anywhere."

He leaned in and pressed a kiss to her damp cheek. "Good. Stay nice and obedient, and everything will be fine, Madison. You'll see."

She waited until he'd left to move. Trystam rushed down the stairs and threw the deadbolt before running to wrap his arms around her legs. "Is he gone, Mommy?"

She sniffled and tried to pull herself together for her son's sake. "Yeah, baby. He's gone." She picked him up and held him close until the trembling in her body and his eased. "He's gone, but we...I need to call Liam, okay?"

"Will he make the bad man stay away?" Trystam whispered, tears filling his eyes when she set him down on a stool in the kitchen.

"I...I don't think so, sweetheart." She wasn't going to tell Liam anything if she didn't have to. She'd cover the bruises with makeup and pray he didn't notice because she couldn't let Alyx take her baby away from her. Even if it meant dealing with the fear and whatever harm he did to her until she could find a way to run far enough to escape his influence, she would. In the meantime, Liam's presence only provoked him. She needed to keep her distance.

Liam picked up on the first ring, concern in his greeting. "Maddie, what is it? You never call me this late."

She almost broke down then and there at the sound of his warm, deep voice, but she held it together. "I...I called to tell you I need a few days off."

"Of course," he agreed, but the concern in his tone sharpened. "Why? What's going on?"

"I need space," she whispered, eyeing her son's confused

expression. "I don't...I don't want to go any further with this, Liam. I need time to figure out how to go back to just being your employee."

The other side of the line was silent for a long time.

"Liam? I...I'm sorry."

"Don't be," he murmured tightly. "Just tell me one thing. Is this because of him? Lie to me, baby girl, and you won't like the consequences."

She almost laughed at the absurdity of the threat. He wouldn't be anything to her after she ended things, let alone someone who could offer consequences for the lie. But she also couldn't bear to lie to him. "Yes, but Liam, please don't do anything. He's your client..."

"Not as of tonight. I had a call from the investigators on the case. He's in no danger now. They've caught the men responsible."

"S-so he can go home?" Her stomach knotted with fear. If Alyx could go home, then that meant he could file that motion any day now. He'd probably file it the moment he was back in the office.

"Yes. You don't sound happy about that. What's going on, Madison?" His voice turned stern. "Do you need me to come over there and deal with this, or are you going to tell me now?"

The dam burst. Everything was just too much. She broke down into tears in front of her son with Liam on the line.

He sighed. "I'll be there in twenty minutes, Maddie. Talk to me while I drive, sweetheart?"

She tried to regain control as Trystam started crying too. "I'm f-fine."

"No, you are not." His voice brooked no argument.

She heard the quiet purr of his car's engine turning on, and then the garage door followed it. "Liam, I mean it." She tried to sound more stern, panic adding to her stress and the quiver in her voice. If Alyx found out Liam had come over here, he'd file the motion for full custody, not just partial. She didn't know if he could actually win it after so many years, but she didn't want to take the risk. "I just want space. I don't want to be with you." Her voice hitched on the last word.

Trystam continued to sob at the counter. "Mommy, I want daddy here. Liam. I want him."

Her heart broke just a little more as a second round of her own tears began. Liam wasn't just embedded in her heart; he was entwined into Trystam's too. "I know, baby, but..."

"Put me on speaker, Maddie."

She hesitated. "Liam..."

"Madison Hayes, speakerphone, right now." His voice barked at her through the phone.

Shivering at the steel in his voice, she nodded before remembering he couldn't see her and offered a soft, "Okay." She clicked the speaker button.

"Trystam?" Liam's voice came through the speaker now, softer than it had been. "What happened, kiddo?"

"He hurt Mommy," Trystam sobbed.

Maddie sucked in a sharp breath. "Trystam!"

"Thank you for being honest, little guy." He cleared his throat. "Madison, did I or did I not ask you what was wrong?"

"You d-did."

Trystam rubbed at his tears, sniffling. "Are you coming to stay with us?"

"Yeah, kiddo. I'll be there in a few minutes, but I also need to speak with your Mommy and with the...the man who hurt her. Is he still hanging around?"

"He's gone," Maddie ventured softly. "But Liam...you don't know what's at stake."

"He said he was going to take me away," Trystam howled with a fresh burst of tears. "I don't want to go with him."

"No one's taking you anywhere." Liam's voice hardened with rage. "Maddie, did he threaten to take Trystam?"

Her shoulders sagged, and tears blurred her vision.

"Madison?" Liam pressed.

"Yes," she whispered.

"Take me off speakerphone."

She obeyed with a quiet whimper. "L-liam, he told me you had to go, or he'd...he'd take Trystam permanently."

"He's not taking anything, and I'm going to kill him for this." His tone had gone from angry to deadly now that Trystam couldn't hear. "You're going to stay there. I will come to get you both when I've dealt with him. Do you understand?"

"I...you'll just make him angry."

"I'm going to make him terrified to cross me or touch either of you ever again," Liam snapped. "He's going to learn he's not the only one with connections, even if I have to call in a few favors to make him disappear for a vacation in some deep, dark hole for a while. Nobody gets away with hurting women and children on my watch, especially not *my* woman or a kid I love like a son."

"But—"

"Enough, Madison. I won't be swayed by this. He's leaving town, and there won't be any custody motion. We'll chat about hiding things like this when I get back, and then we'll talk about what you really want and what I want for our future, baby girl. What you are not going to do is leave the house or answer the door until I call to tell you it's safe. Do you understand?"

"Y-yes, sir," she whispered.

"Good girl. Tell Trystam I'll tuck him in when I come over, please." His tone softened. "Make yourself a hot cup of tea, and put on the television to distract yourself until I come home to you, okay?"

"Okay." Her voice was small and sad, but knowing he wasn't leaving her to deal with Alyx alone left a warmth in her stomach that soothed the knots, though it did nothing for the fire in her face or wrist.

"And ice whatever he did. I assume it isn't bad enough for the ER?"

"No."

"Good. I love you, Maddie. I'll call soon."

With that, he hung up. She shuffled through the motions of settling Trystam in bed and then went to the kitchen to obey his orders. With everything done, she settled in for the long wait until he returned.

Chapter 9

Liam tracked down Alyx into a local bar downtown. News of the man's freedom had traveled quickly, and his men had let him go with glee when he announced he was celebrating before he headed home. Headed home to file that motion for custody, no doubt. He stalked into the busy bar and located Alyx at the bar, already looking a little tipsy.

Grabbing the man by the shoulder, he shot the bartender—a man he'd known for a few years since he'd helped the man's son out of a scrape with drug dealers—a nod. "I think he's had enough to drink, don't you?"

The bartender gave him a nervous glance, obviously catching Liam's mood. "Liam...no violence in my bar."

"What about on the sidewalk outside?" he asked.

"You're going to have at him no matter what, aren't you?"

Alyx scoffed and downed the rest of his drink. "Think you can take me?" He took a wild swing at Liam.

Liam decked him in the jaw, sending the man sprawling. He locked eyes with the bartender. "Sorry. He attacked first. I'll take it outside."

"He deserves it, right?"

"He hurt a woman and frightened her small child. I'll say he deserves it."

The bartender's jaw hardened, and he nodded. He didn't like men who hurt women any more than Liam did. "Make sure he never comes in here or round these parts again, then. Gonna tell the boys around these parts too. They don't take too well to wife-beating cowards."

"Who are you calling a coward?" Alyx growled.

Liam grabbed him by the collar and dragged him through the crowd. "Unless you want his friends to handle you too, you'd better shut up and come outside. I want a few words with you."

Alyx let Liam drag him outside at that, but he swayed drunkenly on the sidewalk and threw himself at Liam the moment he had the chance. Liam pulled his phone from his pocket and switched on the camera, thinking of something one step better than beating the lawyer up. He dodged Alyx's blows for a while until the man noticed the camera on the phone was aiming his way. When Alyx made a move for the phone, Liam stepped out of the drunk's way and let him barrel straight into the dumpster. Then he sent the video to his work laptop as insurance and tucked the phone away.

"All right, playtime is over, Alyx." Liam hauled him up and slammed his back into the brick wall. "No one here is going to help you. If they do, everyone will shrug and say they didn't see anything when the cops show up. I have video of you assaulting and attacking me, and I am going to use it."

Alyx spluttered, face red with anger and drink. "Screw you! You're always screwing up everything around here. My girl...my chance with my son."

"Oh, no. I'm not taking any blame for anything. Well, except maybe the first...but that's beside the point, and she isn't your anything. You screwed things up for yourself the minute you ran off to law school after knocking her up. I was the one who was there for her. *I* helped change that kid's diapers, ran him to school when she was too worn down to do it, made sure she could make rent every month, and babysat when she had tough shifts. When she lost her job, *I* offered her a job so I could support her without making her feel like she was a burden because *you* didn't do your job way back then! She is her own woman, but as near as she's anybody's, she's mine because I take the time to care and be there. I am the one she called crying after you hurt and terrorized her, and I am the one her son cried for because you scared him half to death."

"I wasn't trying to scare him," Alyx muttered darkly.

"Well, too bad. You did. There'll be no more talk about custody, period, Alyx. She and that kid are under my protection. You file that motion, and the judge gets this video. How long do you think your career lasts after that? Let alone a custody battle? You're not getting your hands on that kid or on her ever again. I catch you hanging around Maddie or Trystam ever again, and I'm going to call in favors to make sure you're buried so deep under legal crap that you never practice law again, let alone make it out of the hole they'll dump you in. Do you understand?"

Alyx glowered at him. Liam glared back, unmoved. Maybe he was used to intimidating other men, but Liam wasn't other men, and his woman's safety, as well as that of a boy he'd come to consider a son, was at stake. When Alyx didn't answer, he shook the man. "Do you understand, or do I need to start making calls now?"

Alyx paled and shook his head. "I get it. I get it! I'll go."

"Good. I'll drive you to a hotel outside of town. You're not staying in my company's safe house any longer." He dragged the whining, pleading excuse of a man to his car and shoved him into the passenger's seat. "Puke on it, and I'll be sending a cleaner's bill too."

***

Liam parked in Maddie's driveway with both relief and nerves warring with one another. Now that Alyx was out of the way, he had to know what she really wanted, whether she saw a future with him. Things had been going so well the past few weeks, and he was certain she wanted him, but he was less certain if she would marry him, and he was playing for keeps, not just a few years.

He called her as he climbed out of the car, the relief winning out at the sound of her sleepy hello. "Maddie, baby, it's me. You can open the door."

He'd just made it to the stoop when she flung the door open and threw herself at him. He caught her before she could topple both of them over and held her close, fingers tangled in her hair as he pressed her to his chest. The realization that he could have lost her tonight if Alyx had kept going hit him in the gut, and he tightened his grip as a wave of anger, relief, and belated panic washed over him. She trembled against him, and he felt her tears soaking through the thin t-shirt he wore. He continued to cradle her close as they stood on her doorstep. When her trembling turned to a shiver, he scooped her up in his arms and took her inside, kicking the door shut.

With the warm light from the living room lamp spilling over her face, he could see the purple and blue bruise coming up on her right cheek, and the anger surged once more. He should've hit Alyx a few more times before he'd dragged him out of the bar. The man deserved that and so much more. Reaching out, he traced his fingers over the bruising gently. "I'm sorry I wasn't here to stop him, Maddie."

She leaned into his touch, closing her eyes. "You're here now, aren't you?"

"Yes. And he's gone. You'll never have to worry about him again. If he ever tries to challenge for custody of Trystam, he'll lose everything. One drunk rage and a few swings caught on camera sealed that fate for him. I doubt he'll risk everything to take Trystam away from you."

When she opened her eyes, tears shone there. "You really got rid of him for me?"

"I did. You make it sound like I committed a murder for you."

He forced a smile. "All I did was run him out of town and take a few swings of my own after he started it."

She threw her arms around his neck and burrowed her face into his shoulder. "I don't know how I managed to get a guy so perfect," she mumbled. "I don't deserve it."

He landed a gentle smack on her butt. "Hey. No self-degradation. If I'm not about to let anyone hurt you, then I'm also not going to have *you* hurting you, even if it's just verbal. You are smart, pretty, and big-hearted, Maddie. You do deserve to be loved. You don't deserve the way Alyx treated you, and I'm going to make sure you know it." He softened his tone. "If you'll let me, that is."

She nodded, pressing closer. "I'm sorry I lied on the phone," she whispered. "I was scared. He'd threatened to...to take Trystam, and I was terrified if I let you help, he might do it."

Liam snuggled her into his chest and laid down on the sofa, grabbing the blanket from where she'd left it on the floor and settling it over both of them. He brushed her hair off her tear-stained cheeks with a sigh. "Someday, you're going to learn to trust me completely. But for now, I'll be glad you called and that you obeyed me about the speakerphone so your son could do the rest. He's a brave little kid."

"Yeah. Smart too...he knew to talk even though I was too scared to."

"Yup. He's a bright one." Liam rubbed her back gently. "Are you all right?"

"I am now that you're here." She lifted her head to look up at him. "You said you needed to ask me something?"

He nodded. "I want to know if you see yourself marrying me, Maddie. If you don't, we'll end this here. I'm not going to stay in a romantic relationship with a woman who doesn't want me. If you do, but you need time, I'm going to ask, but I'm not going to push to set a date. It's up to you. Either way, I'm going to remain the same friend you've had for years."

Her lower lip quivered. "You're really going to ask?"

"Is that bad?"

"No. I just don't want to be asked like this."

He chuckled. "Is that a roundabout way of saying yes?"

She smiled, too, despite her exhaustion and all she'd been through. "You have to ask properly, or I'm not saying anything either way."

"Fine, but I'm not waiting to get my answer, Madison Hayes. Will you marry me?"

She laid her head back on his chest. "Yes, I'll marry you. But you'd better propose when I've had time to get over what happened tonight. I want something romantic."

"This isn't romantic?"

That earned him a half-hearted smack. "No, you big idiot...Chocolates and a movie or snuggling under the stars are romantic. A proposal after you've beat a guy up on my behalf is...is..."

"Endearing? Sweet? Spectacular?" he offered teasingly.

"Okay, kind of endearing," she mumbled in agreement. "But not romantic. Ask properly, please?"

"Anything you want, baby girl. Now, let's get you to bed. It's been a difficult day." He sat up, ignoring her sleepy protests, and wrapped her in the blanket. Then he scooped her up and took her to her room. "I have to say goodnight to Trystam. You change for bed. I'll be back."

He slipped out, giving her some space to settle while he went to say goodnight to Trystam. The little boy was already asleep, but he stirred just enough to say goodnight when Liam kissed him on the forehead and pulled the blanket up to tuck it around the boy.

Promise kept, he returned to Maddie's side to find her curled up in bed, still in her t-shirt but missing the jeans, and sound asleep.

Shaking his head with a tired smile, he climbed in beside her and pulled the coverlet up to cover them both before falling asleep with her tucked into his arms.

Epilogue

Eight months later

Maddie walked down the aisle between the seats with a resplendent smile. She didn't have family to give her away, but she walked with a straight back and never wavered, her gaze fixed on him and Trystam, who stood with the rings beside him. Liam had never seen her look as radiant as she did now, with the Caribbean sun shining down on her dirty blond curls and picking out the strands of strawberry blonde, gold, and brown that wove together to showcase the full array of shades her hair held. The dress she wore was simple and elegant. The train hooked up to keep it from dragging in the sand. It hugged her hips in all the right places, and he offered an approving smile as she finally reached him and placed her hands in his.

Jessica was already dabbing at tears from her place in the first row, and his own mother was also crying. He turned his focus to Maddie and the minister with a softer smile, his own joy at having her here before him to become his wife growing as the reality finally sank in. She'd be his in name after this, not just in spirit and body. This would cement their bond in front of all of their family and friends and make Trystam his son officially as well.

The little boy stood proudly in his blue suit, holding the pillow with the rings and grinning at both of them. He'd barely contained his excitement when Liam had told him he could call Liam daddy for real at school after today. His eyes had grown wide when the plane had touched down, and they'd made the drive to the beach resort of the destination wedding. The kid had never seen anything so grand in his life, and Liam was glad he was able to both give the experience and witness his soon-to-be stepson take delight in it. The day wouldn't have been complete without Trystam.

The minister finished his short speech and launched into the vows ceremony. Maddie clutched his hands more tightly, smiling through a veil of tears as she did so. When it came time to speak her vows, however, she said them clearly, her voice never wavering. He said his in turn, and they exchanged rings.

Most of the ceremony had passed in a blur of nerves, excitement, and awe, but everything sharpened into focus when the minister told him he could kiss his bride. He dipped Maddie back and claimed her mouth with his, knowing this was only the first of many, a promise of what would come when he had her to himself. And he had a lifetime to show her what being his really meant because now she was truly and fully his.

Until death did them part, he fully intended to show Madison Hayes what it meant to be fully and completely cherished.

- THE END -

If you enjoyed *Ex-Military Billionaire Daddy*, take a look at a sneak peek of the next book in the series: *Doctor Billionaire Daddy*.

Prologue

Lanie Cooperson was not a woman accustomed to being laughed at or treated in a casually sexual manner that invited a sexual harassment claim. Sitting here in the office of renowned surgeon Chad Gatlin, however, she found herself face to face with both unusual circumstances. She scowled at the man she'd been admiring from the observation deck of the OR only moments earlier and crossed her arms over her chest.

His gaze dropped to her breasts despite the scrubs' modest neckline and her clear irritation with him. "You don't have to be so uptight, Lanie. On my staff, we work hard, and we play hard. The OR is where your seriousness belongs. Outside those walls, we're all well-acquainted and do not need formalities. You'll learn that soon enough."

"My eyes are up here, sir." She kept her voice level despite her rising anger. His behavior reminded her far too much of Kaiden's roving eyes before his cheating and her subsequent break up with him forced her out of her fast track to head nurse. That was how she'd come to be sitting in this chair, to begin with, and she didn't want a repeat. Even though she already loathed Chad Gatlin with every fiber of her being, she planned on sucking up as much as possible while maintaining her dignity. She intended to make head nurse somewhere. If it didn't happen on his staff in this department, it could happen in another surgeon's department as long as she didn't let him derail her career, just like her involvement with Kaiden had done. "I'm not interested in becoming 'well-acquainted' with you if that means what I presume it does."

He cocked a brow and leaned back in his chair with a sly smile. "What do you think it means, Lanie?"

"Miss Cooperson," she corrected quietly. "And I think your reputation precedes you, in numerous ways, Mr. Gatlin."

"Does it now? Do tell."

"The head nurse warned me that you were a notorious womanizer. You've slept your way through all the nurses on your staff and some of the junior doctors in the department too. Some outside of it as well, if the rumors can be believed. I don't believe in relying on rumors, so I suppose we'll stick to saying you've slept your way through most of *your* department."

"And you have a problem with that." He tented his fingers and eyed her curiously.

"Is that a question you'd like an answer to or a mere statement of fact?" she quipped back.

He grinned slowly. "A question I'd like you to answer, Miss Cooperson."

"I don't care who you sleep with on your staff." Oh, but she did. She despised him for doing it. The only people that ranked close to cheats on her list of human waste were philandering playboys like Chad. She just wouldn't say that. "I admire your work in the OR and the tight ship you run there. I watched you perform your last surgery today. It was nicely done."

His grin broadened. "I make it a point to demand nothing but perfection in my OR. You seem like you'll fit in there, at least."

But not in his department as a whole? "Is sleeping with you a requirement to work on your staff, Mr. Gatlin?"

He chuckled and shook his head. "Now, Miss Cooperson, that would open me up to a lawsuit. I might even risk losing my job. Letting me have you is not a requirement to work for me, but most women eventually give in to my charm and allure."

"Only fools, gold diggers, and the incredibly naïve would give in to a man who will never respect them for it, Mr. Gatlin," she murmured. "I am none of those things."

A startled laugh spilled from him. "Are you mocking me, madam?"

"Is that how you perceive it?" She arched a brow. "Perhaps I am merely insulting your entire staff for being foolish or conniving enough to sleep with you and hope for something of it."

"Would you sleep with me merely for the experience, then?" He eyed her from beneath thick, dark lashes. "Is it the idea of doing it and falsely hoping for a happily-ever-after that makes you mad? Or do you simply dislike that women would be willing to sleep with me even if I didn't offer anything but that one night with me?"

She stiffened. "I think this conversation should be over. Let's leave it at 'I respect your work' and ignore how I feel about your personal life or your choice to mix pleasure and business, Mr. Gatlin."

He stood and strolled around the desk, stopping a scant inch from her and pressing his hip into the desk, hands in pockets. "I think you're just a little green, Miss Cooperson," he murmured in a low, silky voice. "You know, you might give me a chance before you judge me. On pleasure or on business."

"You'll only have a chance on the second, sir. May I be excused now to report to the head nurse?"

He leaned in and took hold of her chin, tipping her face up toward his. "I have a reputation to uphold. Are you threatening to cost me that reputation, love? You should know I don't take threats lightly and never lose once I start playing. Do you want to play knowing that?"

She pushed his hand away with a tight smile. "I think you will keep your hands off me unless I invite it because you don't want a lawsuit or, worse yet, jail time. I'll see you in the OR, Mr. Gatlin." Rising, she picked up her purse and strode out the door, leaving him to think what he would. Whatever she did or did not accomplish here, she was going to make sure she never ended up as another notch on Gatlin's belt.

Will Chad ever change to be the man deserving of Lanie? Will Lanie trust his intentions when Chad pursues an official relationship with her or let her past haunt her budding new love?

Book 4 is available on Amazon now!

Printed in Great Britain
by Amazon

15419505R00048